Revised 2nd Edition

Elegant Glassware
of the
Depression Era

By Gene Florence

[signature: Gene Florence]

COLLECTOR BOOKS
A Division of Schroeder Publishing Co., Inc.

The current values in this book should be used only as a guide. They are not intended to set prices, which vary from one section of the country to another. Auction prices as well as dealer prices vary greatly and are affected by condition as well as demand. Neither the Author nor the Publisher assumes responsibility for any losses that might be incurred as a result of consulting this guide.

Additional copies of this book may be ordered from:

COLLECTOR BOOKS
P.O. Box 3009
Paducah, Kentucky 42001
or
Gene Florence
P.O. Box 22186
Lexington, Kentucky 40522

@$19.95 Add $1.00 for postage and handling.

Copyright: Bill Schroeder, Gene Florence, 1985
ISBN: 0-89145-310-5

This book or any part thereof may not be reproduced without the written consent of the Author and Publisher

LAST MINUTE BULLETIN

As I write this (April, 1985), some of my concerns expressed in this book have come to pass. The moulds at Imperial are being sold and are scattering to the winds, even as far as Germany. Information on patterns in this book are as follows:

CAMBRIDGE: Only Caprice is drastically affected. The National Cambridge Club has obtained some of the moulds and I have tried to get a list from them without success. They do not know what they have bought at this time. I do know that Summit Art Glass Co. of Ravenna, Ohio, is making eight different pieces of Caprice right now, including the quarter-pound butter dish in blue. These are original moulds, so beware!

HEISEY: All moulds in existence were bought by the National Heisey Club so all Heisey patterns in this book are safe from reproduction.

IMPERIAL: Moulds of Candlewick have gone in many directions with Mirror Images of Lansing, Michigan, obtaining approximately 200 of them. According to the owner of Mirror Images, Viking Glass will make Candlewick for him but there are no plans to make it in crystal now. Look for colored Candlewick to appear in the future. The moulds of Cape Cod have been retained by Lancaster Colony. It is doubtful that they will compete with their own lines using these.

Subscribe to a monthly publication (page 158) to keep up with late breaking developments. I wish I could tell you more, but this is all I could find out before going to press.

FOREWORD

"Elegant" glassware, as defined in this book, refers to the hand made and etched glassware that was sold in the department stores and jewelry stores during the Depression era through the 1950's as opposed to the dime store and give-away glass that is known as Depression Glass.

The rapid growth of collecting "Elegant" glassware has been phenomenal and many dealers who wouldn't touch that crystal stuff a few years ago are stocking up on as much "Elegant" as basic Depression Glass.

The success of the first book of three years ago has spawned this second edition. However, some technical problems regarding book size have caused the omission of some patterns included in the previous book. I will see that these are included in my next edition of *Collector's Encyclopedia of Depression Glass*.

I hope you enjoy this book; and I hope you will feel the many hours of effort it's taken to give you the best book possible on "Elegant" glassware were well spent.

PRICING

ALL PRICES IN THIS BOOK ARE RETAIL PRICES FOR MINT CONDITION GLASSWARE. This book is intended to be only A GUIDE TO PRICES. There are regional price differences which cannot be reasonably dealt with herein.

You may expect dealers to pay from thirty to fifty percent less than the prices quoted. My personal knowledge of prices comes from my experience of selling glass in my Grannie Bear Antique Shop in Lexington, from my traveling to and selling at shows in various parts of the United States, and immediately prior to the pricing of this book, from attending the Fostoria, Cambridge and Heisey shows. I readily admit to soliciting price information from persons I know to be expert in these various fields so as to provide you with the latest, most accurate pricing information possible. However, final pricing judgment is mine; so, for any errors (or praises), the buck stops here.

MEASUREMENTS

All measurements are from factory catalog lists. It has been my experience that the actual measurements may vary slightly from those listed, so don't be unduly concerned over slight variations.

ACKOWLEDGEMENTS

There are always numerous people behind the scenes of a book without whose help and encouragement the book would never be done. However, many of the people behind this book have gone above and beyond friendship, or even belief, to see that this work made it to press -- and on time! They have given unstintingly of their time, their glassware, and the knowledge of their special fields of interest. They have helped pack and unpack boxes upon boxes of glass; they have sorted and arranged; they've stayed up nights after grueling show dates to discuss, sort, compile and suggest prices for various items. Much as my ego would like to swell thinking they did all this for me, I have to acknowledge that their driving inspiration was YOU, the public. They each wanted a book of this type available to you, hopefully a good book, filled with information about the better glassware. That's what we all wanted. I hereby acknowledge with much gratitude their efforts in behalf of us all! They include the following beautiful people: Dick and Pat Spencer; Yvonne Spencer Heil; Charles and Cecelia Larsen; Hank and Debbie Pugliese; Austin and Shirley Hartsock; George and Veronica Sionakides; Lynn Welker; Gary and Sue Clark; John and Judy Bine; Marilyn and Wayne Ring; Charles "Chuck" Bails; Nadine Pankow; Ralph Leslie; Wayne Pike; Lucille Kennedy; O. J. Scherschligt and Randall Moles.

For the sheer "slave" labor involved in the photography and setting up pictures, I thank our assembly line personnel: Dick Spencer, Charles Larsen, Steve Quertermous, Jane Fryberger, Chuck Bails, Dan Klaver and Cathy Florence. The photography work was done by Dana Curtis of Curtis and Mays Studio in Paducah, Kentucky.

Family, especially, need to be acknowledged, particularly my Mom, "Grannie Bear", who spent weeks washing, packing, and listing glass in a semblance of order for the photography session; then there are Charles and Sib, "Grampaw", and Chad and Marc who keep home operating and animals alive in our absences and who generally pitch in and do whatever needs doing.

I must make particular mention of my wife, Cathy, who has endured all the long years of research, travel, packing and unpacking, both the glassware and me; and who now has gotten even with me by roping me into photographing quilts for her own book, *Collecting Quilts* which, though just published, is getting some great reviews. I am now learning how being "the author's mate" feels!

Few people are in a position to really appreciate all the WORK that goes into writing a book; and even I underestimated this task. This book was no easier than the first and we are only beginning to scratch the surface of "Elegant" glassware.

INDEX

INDEX BY COMPANY

AMERICAN, Line #2056, Fostoria Glass Company, 1915 - Present

Colors: crystal; some amber, blue, green, yellow in late 1920's; white, red currently

A surge in collecting American began with the announcement that Fostoria would no longer make handmade glassware. For some reason, the American public arrived in busses at the outlet stores in Ohio and West Virginia, but Fostoria continues to make around 25 different pieces today. American is molded and not handmade!

I have tried to show as many of the unusual pieces as I could this time. Note the perforated flower pot and the ring holder on page 7. On page 9 you can see the elusive crescent salad plate (named from its shape) in front of the vases. On the left rear of the same photo is the covered straw jar. Many more of these have been "discovered" since it has been determined that these can be put together easily. All you need is the lid from the sugar (sans handles) and a 10″ vase. The one catch is that the vase has to have an inside diameter of at least 3⅝″. Any less than that and the lid will not fit.

The bottom photo on page 9 shows my "What is it?" for this book. Shown in front of the white vase is what appears to be the bottom of a cake stand. I have heard some interesting stories (millinery hat stands) for this piece; so if anyone out there knows for sure, drop me a line.

Please note that RED is currently being made for Fostoria by Viking, and has only been made in the last few years. The vases can still be bought at the outlet stores for less than $9.00.

Items in blue, amber, green and yellow are all elusive except for that 3 footed, 7″ bonbon which sells for about $35.00 in those colors. It will take a little longer to establish prices for other pieces.

All items marked with an asterisk are available at outlet stores in April, 1985, at prices listed.

	Crystal
Appetizer, tray, 10½″ w/6 inserts	177.50
Appetizer, insert, 3¼″	20.00
Ash tray, oval	8.50
Ash tray, 2⅞″, sq.	6.00
Ash tray, 4″, oval	6.50
Ash tray, 5″, sq.	19.50
Ash tray, 5½″, oval	9.00
Basket w/reed handle, 7″ x 9″	67.50
Basket, 10″	25.00*
Bell	57.50
Bottle, condiment or catsup w/stopper	75.00
Bottle, cologne w/stopper, 4½ oz.	45.00
Bottle, water, 44 oz., 9¼″	200.00
Bottle, bitters w/tube, 5¾″, 4½ oz.	47.50
Bottle, cologne w/stopper, 6 oz.	45.00
Bottle, cordial w/stopper, 7¼″, 9 oz.	67.50
Bottle, cologne w/stopper, 8 oz.	50.00
Bowl, banana split	27.50
Bowl, bonbon	12.00
Bowl, finger, 4½″ diam., smooth edge	17.50
Bowl, cream soup, 2 hdld.	40.00
Bowl, 3½″, rose	15.50
Bowl, 3¾″, almond	11.50
Bowl, 4¼″, jelly, 4¼″ h.	15.00
Bowl, 4½″, 1 hdld.	11.00
Bowl, 4½″, 1 hdld., sq.	11.00
Bowl, 4½″, jelly w/cover, 6¾″ h.	20.00
Bowl, 4½″, nappy	15.00
Bowl, 4½″, oval	7.00
Bowl, 4¾″, fruit	12.50
Bowl, 5″, 1 hdld., tri-corner	11.00
Bowl, 5″ nappy	7.00*

	Crystal
Bowl, 5″, rose	20.00
Bowl, 5½″, lemon w/cover	30.00
Bowl, 5½″, preserve, 2 hdld., w/cover	50.00
Bowl, 6″, nappy	16.00
Bowl, 6″, olive, oblong	9.00
Bowl, 6½″, wedding w/cover, sq., ped. ft., 8″ h.	67.50
Bowl, 6½″, wedding, sq., ped. ft., 5¼″ h.	40.00
Bowl, 7″, bonbon, 3 ftd.	10.00*
Bowl, 7″, cupped, 4½″ h.	35.00
Bowl, 7″, nappy	21.00
Bowl, 8″, deep	42.50
Bowl, 8″, ftd.	45.00
Bowl, 8″, ftd. 2 hdld. "trophy" cup	35.00
Bowl, 8″, nappy	12.50*
Bowl, 8″, pickle, oblong	13.00
Bowl, 8″, tid bit, flat, 3 ftd.	22.50
Bowl, 8½″, 2 hdld.	13.50*
Bowl, 8½″, boat	7.50*
Bowl, 9″, boat, 2 pt.	10.50*
Bowl, 9″, oval veg.	25.00
Bowl, 9½″, centerpiece	23.00
Bowl, 9½″, 3 pt., 6″ w.	37.50
Bowl, 10″, celery, oblong	14.00
Bowl, 10″, deep	16.75*
Bowl, 10″, float	30.00
Bowl, 10″, oval float	32.50
Bowl, 10″, oval veg., 2 pt.	30.00
Bowl, 10½″, fruit, 3 ftd.	15.00*
Bowl, 11″, centerpiece	40.00
Bowl, 11″, centerpiece, tri-corner	30.00
Bowl, 11″, relish/celery, 3 pt.	30.00

	Crystal		Crystal
Bowl, 11½″, float	45.00	Creamer, tea, 3 oz., 2⅜″ (#2056 ½)	7.50
Bowl, 11½″, fruit, rolled edge, 2¾″ h.	47.50	Creamer, individual, 4¾ oz.	7.50*
Bowl, 11½″, oval float	45.00	Creamer, 9½ oz.	10.50
Bowl, 11½″, rolled edge	37.50	Crushed fruit w/cover & spoon	225.00
Bowl, 11¾″, oval	37.50	Cup, flat	5.00*
Bowl, 12″, boat	16.00*	Cup, ftd. sherbet, 4½ oz., 3½″ h.	11.00
Bowl, 12″, fruit/sm. punch, ped. ft.,		Cup, ftd., 7 oz.	9.00
(Tom & Jerry)	100.00	Cup, punch, flared rim	10.00
Bowl, 12″, lily pond	60.00	Cup, punch, straight edge	9.00
Bowl, 12″, relish "boat", 2 pt.	18.00	Decanter w/stopper, 24 oz., 9¼″ h.	95.00
Bowl, 13″, fruit, shallow	47.50	Dresser set: powder boxes w/covers & tray	175.00
Bowl, 13″, shallow	30.00	Flower pot w/perforated cover, 9½″ diam.;	
Bowl, 14″, punch w/high ft. base (2 gal.)	175.00	5½″ h.	300.00
Bowl, 14″, punch w/low ft. base	150.00	Goblet, #2056, 2½ oz., wine, hex ft.,	
Bowl, 15″, centerpiece, "hat" shape	125.00	4⅜″ h.	10.00
Bowl, 16″, flat fruit, ped. ft.	100.00	Goblet, #2056, 4½ oz., oyster cocktail,	
Bowl, 18″, punch w/low ft. base (3¾ gal.)	225.00	3½″ h.	11.00
Bowl w/cover, 5″	25.00	Goblet, #2056, 4½ oz., sherbet, flared,	
Box, w/cover, puff, 3⅛″ x 2¾″	85.00	4⅜″ h.	10.00
Box, w/cover, handkerchief, 5⅝″ x 4⅝″	100.00	Goblet, #2056, 4½ oz., fruit, hex ft.,	
Box, w/cover, hairpin, 3½″ x 1¾″	75.00	4¾″ h.	10.00
Box, w/cover, jewel, 5¼″ x 2¼″	75.00	Goblet, #2056, 5 oz., low ft. sherbet, flared,	
Box, w/cover, jewel, 2 drawer, 4¼″ x 3¼″	225.00	3¼″ h.	10.00
Box, w/cover, glove, 9½″ x 3½″	125.00	Goblet, #2056, 6 oz., low ft. sundae,	
Butter, w/cover, rnd, plate 7¼″	100.00	3⅛″ h.	10.00
Butter, w/cover, ¼ lb.	13.50	Goblet, #2056, 7 oz., claret, 4⅞″ h.	11.00
Candelabrum, 6½″, 2-lite, bell base		Goblet, #2056, 9 oz., low ft., 4⅜″ h.	12.00
w/bobeche & prisms	100.00	Goblet, #2056, 10 oz., hex ft. water,	
Candle lamp, 8½″, w/chimney, candle		6⅞″ h.	11.00
part, 3½″	110.00	Goblet, #2056, 12 oz., low ft. tea,	
Candlestick, twin, 4⅛″ h., 8½″ spread	25.00	5¾″ h.	11.00
Candlestick, 2″, chamber	7.50	Goblet, #2056½, 4½ oz., sherbet,	
Candlestick, 3″, rnd. ft.	13.50*	4½″ h.	10.00
Candlestick, 4⅜″″, 2-lite, rnd. ft.	30.00	Goblet, #2056½, 5 oz., low sherbet,	
Candlestick, 6″, octagon ft.	20.00	3½″ h.	10.00
Candlestick, 6½″, 2-lite, bell base	50.00	Goblet, #5056, 1 oz., cordial,	
Candlestick, 6½″, round ft.	150.00	3⅛″ w/plain bowl	27.50
Candlestick, 7″, sq. column	90.00	Goblet, #5056, 3½ oz., claret,	
Candlestick, 7¼″, "Eiffel" tower	90.00	4⅝″ w/plain bowl	14.00
Candy box w/cover, 3 pt.	55.00	Goblet, #5056, 3½ oz., cocktail,	
Candy w/cover, ped. ft.	15.00*	4″ w/plain bowl	14.00
Cheese (5¾″ compote) & cracker		Goblet, #5056, 4 oz., oyster cocktail,	
(11½″ plate)	50.00	3½″ w/plain bowl	10.00
Cigarette box w/cover, 4¾″	30.00	Goblet, #5056, 5½ oz., sherbet,	
Coaster, 3¾″	4.50	4⅛″ w/plain bowl	10.00
Comport, 4½″ jelly	8.00*	Goblet, #5056, 10 oz., water,	
Comport, 5″, jelly, flared	12.00	6⅛″ w/plain bowl	12.00
Comport, 6¾″, jelly w/cover	30.00	Hair receiver, 3″ x 3″	55.00
Comport, 8½″	35.00	Hat, 2⅛″, (sm. ash tray)	12.00
Comport, 9½″	37.50	Hat, 3″	22.50
Comport w/cover, 5″	22.50	Hat, 4″	42.50
Cookie jar w/cover, 8⅞″ h.	225.00	Hurricane lamp, 12″ complete	135.00

AMERICAN, Line #2056, Fostoria Glass Company, 1915 - Present (continued)

	Crystal		Crystal
Hurricane lamp base	42.50	Salver, 10″, rnd., ped. ft. (cake stand)	48.00
Ice bucket w/tongs	50.00	Salver, 11″, rnd. ped. ft. (cake stand)	22.00*
Ice dish for 4 oz. crab or 5 oz. tomato liner	30.00	Sauce boat & liner	67.50
Ice dish insert	5.00	Saucer	5.00*
Ice tub w/liner, 5⅝″	47.50	Set: 2 jam pots w/tray	95.00
Ice tub w/liner, 6½″	50.00	Set: decanter, 6 - 2 oz. whiskeys on	
Jam pot w/cover	40.00	10½″ tray	200.00
Jar, pickle w/pointed cover, 6″ h.	125.00	Set: toddler, w/baby tumbler & bowl	45.00
Marmalade w/cover & chrome spoon	35.00	Set: youth, w/bowl, hdld. mug, 6″	
Mayonnaise, div.	7.50*	plate	55.00
Mayonnaise w/ladle, ped. ft.	35.00	Set, condiment: 2 oils, 2 shakers, mustard	
Mayonnaise w/liner & ladle	32.50	w/cover & spoon w/tray	175.00
Molasses can, 11 oz., 6¾″ h., 1 hdld.	100.00	Shaker, 3″, ea.	9.50
Mug, 5½ oz., "Tom & Jerry", 3¼″ h.	25.00	Shaker, 3½″, ea.	5.50*
Mug, 12 oz., beer, 4½″ h.	32.50	Shaker, 3¼″, ea.	9.50
Mustard w/cover	30.00	Shakers w/tray, individual, 2½″	15.00
Napkin ring	5.00	Shrimp bowl, 12¼″	187.50
Oil, 5 oz.	25.00	Spooner, 3¾″	32.50
Oil, 7 oz.	35.00	Strawholder, 10″ w/cover	225.00
Picture frame	5.50*	Sugar, tea, #2056½, 2¼″	7.50
Pitcher, ½ gal. w/ice lip, 8¼″, flat		Sugar, hdld, 3¼″ h.	7.50*
bottom	50.00	Sugar shaker	30.00
Pitcher, ½ gal., 8″, ftd.	62.50	Sugar w/cover, no hand., 6¼″ (cover fits	
Pitcher, 1 pt., 5⅜″, flat	27.50	strawholder)	50.00
Pitcher, 2 pt., 7¼″, ftd.	50.00	Sugar w/cover, 2 hdld.	17.50
Pitcher, 3 pt., 8″, ftd.	47.50	Syrup, 6½ oz., #2056½, Sani-cut server	40.00
Pitcher, 3 pt., w/ice lip, 6½″, ftd., "fat"	50.00	Syrup, 6 oz., non pour screw top,	
Pitcher, 1 qt., flat	20.00*	5¼″ h.	85.00
Plate, cream soup liner	8.00	Syrup, 10 oz., w/glass cover & 6″	
Plate, 6″, bread & butter	8.00	liner plate	85.00
Plate, 7″, salad	8.50	Syrup, w/drip proof top	25.00
Plate, 7½″ x 4⅜″ crescent salad	37.50	Toothpick	17.50
Plate, 8″, sauce liner, oval	22.50	Tray, cloverleaf for condiment set	87.50
Plate, 8½″, salad	8.00*	Tray, tid bit, w/question mark metal hand.	27.50
Plate, 9″, sandwich (sm. center)	14.00	Tray, 5″ x 2½″, rect.	15.00
Plate, 9½″, dinner	12.00*	Tray, 6″ oval, hdld.	30.00
Plate, 10″, cake, 2 hdld.	16.00	Tray, 6½″ x 9″ relish, 4 part	47.50
Plate, 10½″ sandwich (sm. center)	16.00	Tray, 9½″, service, 2 hdld.	27.50
Plate, 11½″, sandwich (sm. center)	16.00	Tray, 10″, muffin (2 upturned sides)	25.00
Plate, 12″, cake, 3 ftd.	22.50	Tray, 10″, square, 4 part	65.00
Plate, 13½″, oval torte	27.50	Tray, 10″, square	95.00
Plate, 14″, torte	16.75*	Tray, 10½″, cake, w/question mark metal	
Plate, 18″, torte	65.00	hand.	25.00
Plate, 20″, torte	85.00	Tray, 10½″ x 7½″, rect.	65.00
Platter, 10½″, oval	27.50	Tray, 10½″ x 5″, oval, hdld.	37.50
Platter, 12″, oval	40.00	Tray, 10¾″, square, 4 part	85.00
Platter, 14″, oval	65.00	Tray, 12″, oval (dresser type)	40.00
Ring holder	100.00	Tray, 12″, sand. w/ctr. handle	32.50
Salad set: 10″ bowl, 14″ torte, wood		Tray, 12″, round	85.00
fork & spoon	67.50	Tray, 13½″, oval ice cream	52.50
Salt, individual	5.00	Tray for sugar & creamer, tab. hdld.,	
Salver, 10″, sq., ped. ft. (cake stand)	58.00	6¾″	9.00

	Crystal		Crystal
Tumbler, hdld. iced tea, 7½"	45.00	Urn, 6", sq., ped. ft.	25.00
Tumbler, #2056, 2 oz., whiskey, 2½" h.	12.50	Urn, 7½", sq., ped. ft.	30.00
Tumbler, #2056, 3 oz., ftd. cone cocktail		Vase, 4½", sweet pea	80.00
2⅞" h.	13.50	Vase, 6", bud, ftd.	8.00*
Tumbler, #2056, 5 oz., ftd. juice, 4¾"	10.00	Vase, 6", bud, flared	8.00*
Tumbler, #2056, 6 oz., flat old fashioned,		Vase, 6", straight side	25.00
3⅜" h.	11.00	Vase, 6½", flared rim	15.00
Tumbler, #2056, 8 oz., flat water, flared,		Vase, 7", flared	67.50
4⅛" h.	12.00	Vase, 8", straight side	40.00
Tumbler, #2056, 9 oz., ftd. water		Vase, 8", flared	77.50
4⅞" h.	12.00	Vase, 8", porch, 5" diam.	175.00
Tumbler, #2056, 12 oz., flat tea, flared		Vase, 8½", bud, flared	20.00
5¼" h.	14.00	Vase, 8½", bud, cupped	20.00
Tumbler, #2056½, 5 oz., straight side		Vase, 9", w/sq. ped. ft.	37.50
juice	13.00	Vase, 9½", flared	95.00
Tumbler, #2056½, 8 oz., straight side		Vase, 10", cupped in top	157.50
water, 3⅞" h.	13.00	Vase, 10", porch, 8" diam.	197.50
Tumbler, #2056½, 12 oz., straight side		Vase, 10", straight side	85.00
tea, 5" h.	13.00	Vase, 10", swung	175.00
Tumbler, #5056, 5 oz., ftd. juice, 4⅛"		Vase, 10", flared	87.50
w/plain bowl	12.00	Vase, 12", straight side	95.00
Tumbler, #5056, 12 oz., ftd. tea, 5½"		Vase, 14", swung	225.00
w/plain bowl	12.00	Vase, 20", swung	275.00

All items marked with an asterisk are available at outlet stores in April, 1985, at prices listed.

APPLE-BLOSSOM, Line #3400, Cambridge Glass Company, 1930's

Colors: blue, pink, green, yellow, crystal, amber

I have had fun looking for different pieces in this pattern. Were there more blue available, I might even get hooked into collecting it myself. If you wish to collect a set, you would be wise to select yellow or crystal since those colors are more prevalent. Pink or green would be more difficult, but they would make a beautiful set! Speaking of pink, be sure to see page 45 under Cleo for a handled relish with both etchings on it.

	Crystal	Colors		Crystal	Colors
Bowl, #3025, ftd. finger w/plate	14.00	25.00	Plate, sandwich, 11½", tab hdld.	12.50	27.00
Bowl, #3130, finger w/plate	12.00	20.00	Plate, sandwich, 12½", 2 hdld.	20.00	32.00
Bowl, 5¼", 2 hdld. bonbon	9.00	15.00	Plate, sq. bread/butter	4.00	8.00
Bowl, 5½", 2 hdld. bonbon	9.00	15.00	Plate, sq. dinner	20.00	40.00
Bowl, 5½", fruit "saucer"	7.00	12.00	Plate, sq. salad	7.00	15.00
Bowl, 6", 2 hdld. "basket"			Plate, sq. service	12.00	25.00
(sides up)	12.00	20.00	Platter, 11½"	20.00	35.00
Bowl, 6", cereal	9.00	17.00	Platter, 13½" rect. w/tab handle	25.00	50.00
Bowl, 9", pickle	10.00	17.50	Salt & pepper, pr.	26.00	85.00
Bowl, 10", 2 hdld.	17.50	30.00	Saucer	2.50	4.00
Bowl, 10", baker	17.50	37.50	Stem, #3025, 7 oz., low fancy ft.		
Bowl, 11", fruit, tab hdld.	17.50	35.00	sherbet	8.00	13.00
Bowl, 11", low ftd.	17.50	35.00	Stem, #3025, 7 oz., high sherbet	9.00	14.00
Bowl, 12", relish, 4 pt.	17.50	37.50	Stem, #3025, 10 oz.	15.00	25.00
Bowl, 12", 4 ftd.	22.50	40.00	Stem, #3130, 1 oz., cordial	35.00	60.00
Bowl, 12", flat	28.00	35.00	Stem, #3130, 3 oz., cocktail	12.50	25.00
Bowl, 12", oval, 4 ftd.	25.00	50.00	Stem, #3130, 6 oz., low sherbet	9.00	18.00
Bowl, 12½", console	17.50	35.00	Stem, #3130, 6 oz., tall sherbet	9.00	17.00
Bowl, 13"	17.50	32.00	Stem, #3130, 8 oz., water	12.00	25.00
Bowl, cream soup w/liner plate	12.00	25.00	Stem, #3135, 3 oz., cocktail	12.50	25.00
Butter w/cover, 5½"	95.00	150.00	Stem, #3135, 6 oz., low sherbet	9.00	16.00
Candelabrum, 3-lite, keyhole	16.50	35.00	Stem, #3135, 6 oz., tall sherbet	9.00	18.00
Candlestick, 1-lite, keyhole	10.00	20.00	Stem, #3135, 8 oz., water	12.00	25.00
Candlestick, 2-lite, keyhole	14.00	30.00	Stem, #3400, 6 oz., ftd. sherbet	9.00	17.50
Candy box w/cover, 4 ftd. "bowl"	35.00	85.00	Stem, #3400, 9 oz., water	10.00	25.00
Cheese (compote) & cracker (11½"			Sugar, ftd.	6.00	15.00
plate)	20.00	40.00	Sugar, tall ftd.	6.00	15.00
Comport, 4", fruit cocktail	11.50	17.50	Tray, 11" ctr. hdld. sand.	20.00	35.00
Comport, 7", tall	17.50	40.00	Tumbler, #3025, 4 oz.	10.00	15.00
Creamer, ftd.	10.00	17.00	Tumbler, #3025, 10 oz.	12.00	25.00
Creamer, tall ftd.	10.00	17.00	Tumbler, #3025, 12 oz.	14.00	27.50
Cup	9.00	20.00	Tumbler, #3130, 5 oz., ftd.	8.00	15.00
Fruit/oyster cocktail, #3025, 4½ oz.	10.00	15.00	Tumbler, #3130, 8 oz., ftd.	11.00	17.50
Mayonnaise w/liner & ladle, (4 ftd.			Tumbler, #3130, 10 oz., ftd.	11.00	20.00
bowl)	22.50	40.00	Tumbler, #3130, 12 oz., ftd.	14.00	25.00
Pitcher, 50 oz., ftd., flattened sides	65.00	110.00	Tumbler, #3135, 5 oz., ftd.	8.00	15.00
Pitcher, 64 oz., #3130	70.00	150.00	Tumbler, #3135, 8 oz., ftd.	10.00	20.00
Pitcher, 64 oz., #3025	70.00	150.00	Tumbler, #3135, 10 oz., ftd.	12.00	20.00
Pitcher, 67 oz., squeezed middle,			Tumbler, #3135, 12 oz., ftd.	12.50	25.00
loop hdld.	85.00	200.00	Tumbler, #3400, 2½ oz., ftd.	10.00	20.00
Pitcher, 76 oz.	70.00	185.00	Tumbler, #3400, 9 oz., ftd.	9.00	15.00
Pitcher, 80 oz., ball	80.00	175.00	Tumbler, #3400, 12 oz., ftd.	12.00	20.00
Pitcher w/cover, 76 oz., ftd., #3135	95.00	200.00	Tumbler, 12 oz., flat (2 styles) - 1 mid		
Plate, 6", bread/butter	4.00	8.00	indent to match 67 oz. pitcher	15.00	30.00
Plate, 6", sq., 2 hdld.	7.00	12.00	Tumbler, 6"	12.50	25.00
Plate, 7½", tea	6.00	10.00	Vase, 5"	17.50	27.50
Plate, 8½"	6.00	10.00	Vase, 6", rippled sides	18.00	35.00
Plate, 9½", dinner	25.00	45.00	Vase, 8", 2 styles	20.00	40.00
Plate, 10", grill	12.00	20.00	Vase, 12", keyhole base w/neck indent	25.00	65.00

Note: See Pages 148-149 for stem identification.

BAROQUE, Line #2496, Fostoria Glass Company, 1936 - 1966

Colors: crystal, "Azure" blue, "Topaz" yellow, green

Oil bottles in each color are shown here. The blue pitcher and oil have turned out to be more elusive than those in yellow. Green candlesticks turned up in Houston last year, but I have not been able to find a console bowl to go with them.

A punch bowl has been found in both crystal and blue but not in yellow. Individual shakers are finally surfacing in color, but not in great numbers.

	Crystal	Blue	Yellow
Ash tray	7.50	14.50	12.50
Bowl, cream soup	8.00	-----	-----
Bowl, ftd. punch	200.00	1250.00	-----
Bowl, 3¾", rose	18.00	35.00	30.00
Bowl, 4", hdld. (3 styles)	8.00	15.00	12.50
Bowl, 5", fruit	9.00	16.00	12.50
Bowl, 6", cereal	10.00	22.50	20.00
Bowl, 6", sq.	8.00	14.00	12.00
Bowl, 6½", 2 pt.	9.00	14.00	12.50
Bowl, 7", 3 ftd.	10.00	20.00	17.50
Bowl, 7½", jelly w/cover	20.00	37.50	30.00
Bowl, 8", pickle	8.00	16.00	13.50
Bowl, 8½", hdld.	12.00	25.00	20.00
Bowl, 9½", veg. oval	17.50	30.00	25.00
Bowl, 10", hdld.	15.00	35.00	30.00
Bowl, 10½", hdld.	17.50	35.00	30.00
Bowl, 10" x 7½"	20.00	-----	-----
Bowl, 10", relish, 3 pt.	17.50	27.50	22.50
Bowl, 11", celery	12.00	22.50	20.00
Bowl, 11", rolled edge	20.00	35.00	30.00
Bowl, 12", flared	21.50	30.00	25.00
Candelabrum, 8¼", 2-lite, 16 lustre	40.00	40.00	35.00
Candelabrum, 9½", 3-lite, 24 lustre	50.00	50.00	42.50
Candle, 7¾", 8 lustre	12.50	25.00	22.50
Candlestick, 4"	8.00	15.00	12.50
Candlestick, 4½", 2-lite	11.00	20.00	17.50
Candlestick, 5½"	9.00	17.50	15.00
Candlestick, 6", 3-lite	15.00	25.00	20.00

BAROQUE, Line #2496, Fostoria Glass Company, 1936 - 1966 (continued)

	Crystal	Blue	Yellow
Comport, 4¾"	9.00	20.00	16.50
Comport, 6½"	8.00	22.00	18.00
Creamer, 3¼", indiv.	6.00	11.00	10.00
Creamer, 3¾", ftd.	7.00	12.00	12.00
Cup	6.50	15.00	11.00
Cup, 6 oz. punch	7.50	15.00	12.50
Ice bucket	22.00	50.00	45.00
Mayonnaise, 5½", w/liner	15.00	35.00	30.00
Mustard w/cover	20.00	40.00	35.00
Oil w/stopper, 5½"	35.00	275.00	225.00
Pitcher, 6½"	150.00	500.00	400.00
Pitcher, 7", ice lip	125.00	475.00	375.00
Plate, 6"	3.00	5.00	4.00
Plate, 7"	4.00	9.00	7.00
Plate, 8"	6.00	11.00	9.00
Plate, 9"	12.00	25.00	23.00
Plate, 10", cake	10.00	21.50	20.00
Plate, 11", ctr. hdld. sand.	14.00	-----	-----
Plate, 14", torte	13.00	27.50	22.50
Platter, 12", oval	15.00	32.50	30.00
Salt & pepper, pr.	25.00	95.00	90.00
Salt & pepper, indiv., pr.	35.00	100.00	90.00
Saucer	2.00	5.00	4.00
Sherbet, 3¾", 5 oz.	8.00	17.50	15.50
Stem, 6¾", 9 oz., water	12.50	22.00	20.00
Sugar, 3", indiv.	5.00	11.00	10.00
Sugar, 3½", ftd.	6.00	11.00	11.00
Tray, 11", oval	10.00	21.50	18.00
Tray for indiv. cream/sugar	6.00	10.00	8.00
Tumbler, 3½", 6½ oz., old fashioned	10.00	20.00	17.50
Tumbler, 3", 3½ oz., ftd. cocktail	9.00	16.00	13.50
Tumbler, 3¾", 5 oz., juice	8.00	22.00	18.00
Tumbler, 4¼", 9 oz., water	12.00	23.50	20.00
Tumbler, 5¾", 14 oz., tea	15.00	30.00	25.00
Vase, 6½"	15.00	35.00	32.50
Vase, 7"	15.00	40.00	37.50

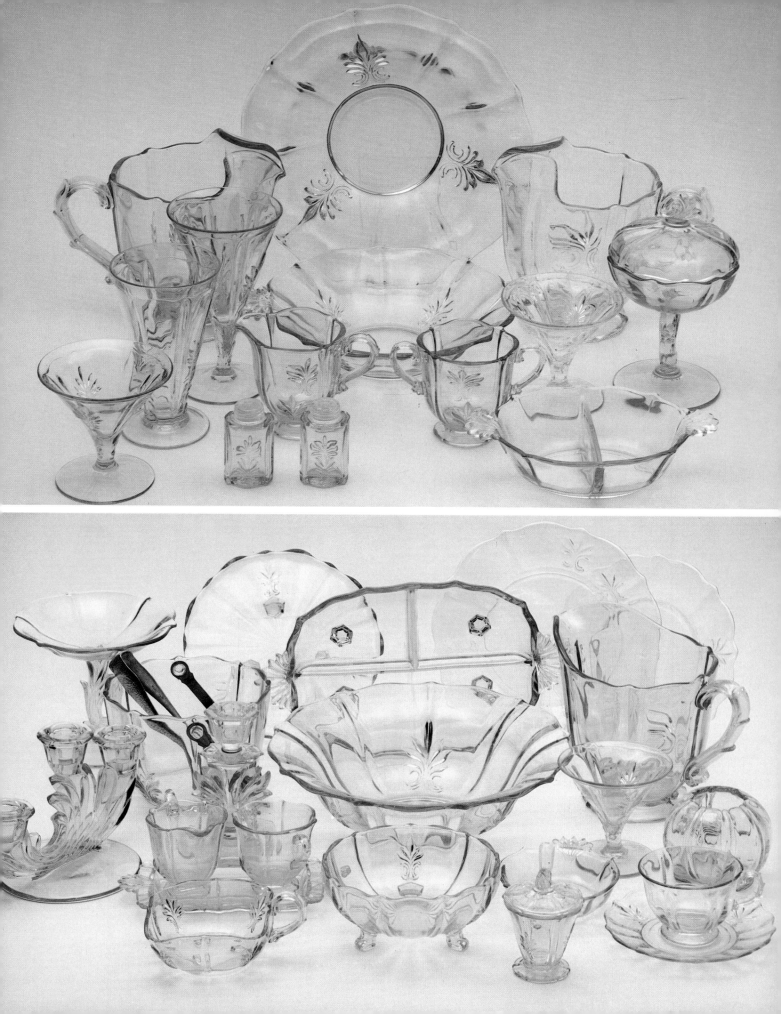

CADENA, Tiffin Glass Company, Early 1930's

Colors: crystal; yellow; some pink

In order to save a few letters this time, . . . yes! there is a chip out of the rim of the pitcher. It is the only one I could find; and naturally, the price was reasonable, so, here it is. I came across a few pieces in pink (including a cordial which I needed for my cordial collection), but the owner placed a much higher value on it than I did. While I am on the subject of pricing, I might add that only two people determine price, buyer and seller. I RECORD what glass is SELLING for at shows and in my shop, and not what is being asked for the glass. Glass can be ADVERTISED at any price, but what it actually sells for is another matter entirely. It is up to you, the purchaser, to determine what it is worth to you. Many times I do not buy glass because the owner thinks it is worth more than I do.

	Crystal	Yellow
Bowl, cream soup	15.00	22.00
Bowl, finger, ftd.	12.00	17.50
Bowl, grapefruit, ftd.	17.50	30.00
Bowl, 6″, hdld.	10.00	15.00
Bowl, 10″, pickle	12.50	20.00
Bowl, 12″, console	22.50	35.00
Candlestick	13.50	20.00
Creamer	15.00	25.00
Cup	15.00	25.00
Goblet, 4¾″, sherbet	15.00	22.00
Goblet, 5¼″, cocktail	17.50	25.00
Goblet, 5¼″, ¾ oz., cordial	30.00	50.00
Goblet, 6″, wine	22.00	32.50
Goblet, 6½″, champagne	17.00	35.00
Goblet, 7½″, water	20.00	27.50
Mayonnaise, ftd. w/liner	25.00	37.50
Oyster cocktail	15.00	22.00
Pitcher, ftd. w/cover	175.00	265.00
Plate, 6″	5.00	8.00
Plate, 7¾″	7.00	12.00
Plate, 9¼″	15.00	30.00
Saucer	4.00	6.00
Sugar	15.00	23.00
Tumbler, 4¼″, ftd. juice	15.00	22.50
Tumbler, 5¼″, ftd. water	17.00	25.00

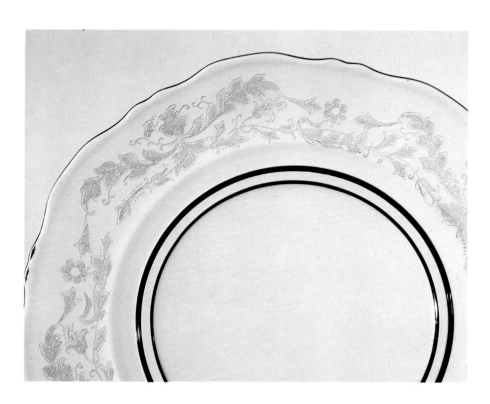

21

CANDLEWICK, Line #400, Imperial Glass Company, 1936 - 1984

Colors: crystal, blue, pink, yellow, black, red, cobalt blue; a few items in color recently

As I write this, there is good news and bad news in collecting Candlewick. The good news is that Candlewick is no longer being made and has skyrocketed in price. The bad news is that no one knows what is going to happen to the moulds now that Imperial is closed and Lancaster Colony is selling to the highest bidder. Subscribe to a current glass publication (page 158) so that you can keep abreast of these happenings. My only hope is that the moulds do not go to some other company who would continue to market Candlewick. I do know that when I visited Imperial while working on the first book, I copied down a list of over 600 Candlewick moulds that were inventoried. How many of these are usable and how many are beyond repair is a big question mark.

The 1947 calendar was bought by a collector out of a desk drawer at the factory during the time that Imperial was trying to save itself from bankruptcy. I might add that a lot of odd, unusual items as well as colors were bought from the basement and the attic during this time. Cobalt blue, red and even black made appearances in quantities never known before. It will take a while for these items to appear on the market and a price to be determined.

See Page 3 For Last Minute Information!

	Crystal		Crystal
Ash tray, 5″	8.00	Bowl, 6″, cottage cheese	15.00
Ash tray, eagle, 6½″	35.00	Bowl, 6″, fruit	10.00
Ash tray, heart, 4½″	8.50	Bowl, 6″, heart w/hand.	20.00
Ash tray, heart, 5½″	12.50	Bowl, 6″, mint	10.00
Ash tray, heart, 6½″	12.50	Bowl, 6″, mint w/hand.	13.00
Ash tray, indiv.	5.00	Bowl, 6″, round	12.00
Ash tray, oblong, 4½″	5.50	Bowl, 6″, round, div.	10.00
Ash tray, round, 2¾″	6.00	Bowl, 6″, 3 ftd.	17.50
Ash tray, round, 4″	6.50	Bowl, 6″, sq.	12.00
Ash tray, square, 3¼″	5.00	Bowl, 6½″, fruit	12.00
Ash tray, square, 4½″	6.50	Bowl, 6½″, relish, 2 pt.	13.50
Ash tray, square, 5¾″	7.00	Bowl, 6½″, 2 hdld.	14.00
Ash tray (nut dish or sugar dip), 2¾″	6.00	Bowl, 7″, round	14.00
Ash tray (or jelly), 4″	5.00	Bowl, 7″, round, 2 hdld.	16.00
Ash tray set, 3 pc. rnd. nest. (crys. or colors)	20.00	Bowl, 7″, relish, sq., div.	17.50
Ash tray set, 3 pc. sq. nesting	20.00	Bowl, 7″, ivy, high, bead ft.	30.00
Ash tray set, 4 pc. bridge (cig. hold at side) .	65.00	Bowl, 7″, lily, 4 ft.	27 50
Basket, 5″, hdld.	32.50	Bowl, 7″, relish	16.00
Basket, 6½″, hdld.	27.50	Bowl, 7″, sq.	15.00
Basket, 11″, hdld.	77.50	Bowl, 7″, sq. relish, div.	15.00
Bell, 4″	25.00	Bowl, 7¼″, rose, ftd. w/crimp edge	37.50
Bell, 5″	32.50	Bowl, 7½″, pickle/celery	15.00
Bottle, bitters w/tube, 4 oz.	40.00	Bowl, 7½″, lily, bead rim, ftd.	27.50
Bowl, bouillon, 3 hdld.	17.50	Bowl, 7½″, belled, (console base)	25.00
Bowl, #3400, finger	12.00	Bowl, 7½″, pickle/celery	15.00
Bowl, #3800, finger	12.00	Bowl, 8″, round	20.00
Bowl, 4½″, nappy, 3 ftd.	15.50	Bowl, 8″, relish, 2 pt.	15.75
Bowl, 4¾″, fruit, 2 hdld.	11.50	Bowl, 8″, cov. veg.	40.00
Bowl, 4¾″, round, 2 hdld.	12.00	Bowl, 8½″, rnd.	22.50
Bowl, 5″, basket, 2 upturned sides	25.00	Bowl, 8½″, nappy, 4 ftd.	30.00
Bowl, 5″, bonbon, hdld.	16.00	Bowl, 8½″, 3 ftd.	25.00
Bowl, 5″, cream soup	13.50	Bowl, 8½″, 2 hdld.	22.50
Bowl, 5″, fruit	8.50	Bowl, 8½″, pickle/celery	15.00
Bowl, 5″, heart	15.00	Bowl, 8½″, relish, div., 2 hdld.	20.00
Bowl, 5″, heart w/hand.	25.00	Bowl, 8½″, relish, 4 pt.	20.00
Bowl, 5″, square	20.00	Bowl, 9″, round	22.50
Bowl, 5½″, heart	10.00	Bowl, 9″, crimp, ftd.	30.00
Bowl, 5½″, jelly w/cover	30.00	Bowl, 9″, sq., fancy crimp edge, 4 ft.	35.00
Bowl, 5½″, sauce	10.00	Bowl, 9″, fruit, low ft.	30.00
Bowl, 6″, baked apple, rolled edge	15.00	Bowl, 9″, heart	40.00

	Crystal		Crystal
Bowl, 9″, heart w/hand.	50.00	Candleholder, flower, 6½″	20.00
Bowl, 10″	22.50	Candleholder, mushroom	18.50
Bowl, 10″, banana	90.00	Candleholder, rolled edge	10.00
Bowl, 10″, belled	25.00	Candleholder, urn, 6″, holders on cir.	
Bowl, 10″, belled, punch base	30.00	ctr. bead	38.50
Bowl, 10″, cupped edge	25.00	Candy box, round, 5½″	22.50
Bowl, 10″, deep, 2 hdld.	22.50	Candy box, sq., 6½″, rnd. lid	37.50
Bowl, 10″, divided, deep, 2 hdld.	22.50	Candy box w/cover, flared, 7″	27.50
Bowl, 10″, fruit, bead stem (like compote)	37.50	Candy box w/cover, partitioned	25.00
Bowl, 10″, heart	30.00	Candy box w/cover, round, 7″	25.00
Bowl, 10″, heart w/hand.	55.00	Candy box w/cover, ftd.	30.00
Bowl, 10″, relish, 3 pt.	20.00	Cigarette box w/cover	17.50
Bowl, 10″, relish, 3 pt., 3 ft.	22.50	Cigarette holder, 3″, bead ft.	20.00
Bowl, 10½″, belled	27.50	Cigarette set: 6 pc., (cigarette box & 4 rect.	
Bowl, 10½″, butter/jam, 3 pt.	42.50	ash trays)	37.50
Bowl, 10½″, flared	25.00	Coaster, 4″	5.00
Bowl, 10½″, oval, flared	25.00	Coaster w/spoon rest	25.00
Bowl, 10½″, salad	25.00	Cocktail, seafood w/bead ft.	20.00
Bowl, 10½″, 3 ft.	27.50	Cocktail set: 2 pc., plate w/indent; cocktail	17.50
Bowl, 10½″, relish, 3 pt.	20.00	Compote, 10″, ftd. fruit, crimped	52.50
Bowl, 11″, celery boat, oval	22.50	Compote, 4½″	12.00
Bowl, 11″, centerpiece, flared	35.00	Compote, 5″, bulbous bead stem	20.00
Bowl, 11″, float, inward rim, ftd.	32.50	Compote, 5½″, bead stem, flared	17.50
Bowl, 11″, oval	22.00	Compote, 5½″, low, plain stem	13.50
Bowl, 11″, oval w/partition	22.50	Compote, 5½″, bead stem	15.00
Bowl, 12″, round	22.50	Compote, 8″, bead stem	22.50
Bowl, 12″, belled	25.00	Compote, ft. oval	35.00
Bowl, 12″, float	25.50	Condiment set:	
Bowl, 12″, hdld.	27.50	4 pc., (2 squat bead ft. shakers,	
Bowl, 12″, oval, flared	20.00	marmalade)	45.00
Bowl, 12″, relish, oblong	22.00	Console sets:	
Bowl, 13″, centerpiece, mushroom	47.50	3 pc. (14″ oval bowl, two 3-lite	
Bowl, 13″, float, 1½″ deep	27.50	candles)	62.50
Bowl, 13½″, relish, 5 pt.	30.00	3 pc. (mushroom bowl, 2 mushroom	
Bowl, 14″, belled	40.00	candles)	67.50
Bowl, 14″, oval	45.00	4 pc. (tall, ft. mushroom bowl, two	
Bowl, 14″, oval, flared	45.00	2-lite candles)	65.00
Butter and jam set, 5 piece	125.00	Creamer, 6 oz., bead handle	7.50
Butter w/cover, rnd, 5½″	22.50	Creamer, indiv. bridge	5.00
Butter w/cover, no beads, California	75.00	Creamer, plain ft.	6.00
Butter w/bead top, ¼ lb.	21.50	Cup, after dinner	17.50
Cake stand, 10″, low foot	45.00	Cup, coffee	8.50
Cake stand, 11″, high foot	50.00	Cup, punch	6.00
Calendar, 1947	75.00	Cup, tea	7.50
Candleholder, signed "Candlewick"	97.50	Decanter w/stopper	70.00
Candleholder, 2-lite	15.00	Deviled egg server, 12″, ctr. hdld.	75.00
Candleholder, 3½″	10.50	Egg cup	25.00
Candleholder, 3½″, w/fingerhold	28.00	Egg cup, bead. ft.	30.00
Candleholder, 3-lite on cir. bead. ctr.	35.00	Fork & spoon, set	17.50
Candleholder, 5″, hdld. w/bowled up base	32.50	Hurricane lamp, 2 pc. candle base	32.50
Candleholder, 5½″	25.00	Hurricane lamp, 3 pc. flared & crimped	
Candleholder, 6½″	27.50	edge globe	75.00
Candleholder, flat	12.50	Ice tub, 5½″ deep, 8″ diam.	37.50
Candleholder, flower, 4″	12.00	Ice tub, 7″, 2 hdld.	42.50
Candleholder, flower, 4½″	12.50	Icer, 2 pc., seafood/fruit cocktail	27.50
Candleholder, flower, 5″, (epergne)	45.00	Icer, 2 pc., seafood/fruit cocktail	
Candleholder, flower, 6″	20.00	#3800 line	27.50

	Crystal		Crystal
Jam set, 5 pc., oval tray w/2 marmalade jars w/ladles	77.50	Plate, 9″, 2 hdld. (sides upturned)	15.00
Jar tower, 3 sect.; jar w/lid, spoon, all on tray	57.50	Plate, 9″, luncheon	12.00
		Plate, 9″, oval salad	14.00
Knife, butter	55.00	Plate, 10″, 2 hdld.	17.00
Ladle, marmalade, 3 bead stem	3.50	Plate, 10″, 2 hdld. crimped	17.00
Ladle, mayonnaise, 6¼″	4.50	Plate, 10″, dinner	22.00
Marmalade set, 3 pc., beaded ft. w/cover & spoon	22.50	Plate, 10″, hdld.	16.00
		Plate, 10½″	17.50
Marmalade set, 3 pc. tall jar, bead ft. lid, spoon	27.50	Plate, 12″	20.00
		Plate, 12″, 2 hdld.	22.50
Marmalade set, 4 pc., liner saucer, jar, lid, spoon	30.00	Plate, 12″, 2 hdld. crimp.	25.00
		Plate, 12″, service	20.00
Mayonnaise set, 2 pc. scoop side bowl, spoon	25.00	Plate, 12½″, cupped edge, torte	25.00
		Plate, 12½″, oval	27.50
Mayonnaise set, 3 pc. hdld. tray/hdld bowl/ladle	27.50	Plate, 13″, cupped edge serving	27.50
		Plate, 14″ birthday cake (holes for candles)	225.00
Mayonnaise set, 3 pc. plate, heart bowl, spoon	30.00	Plate, 14″, 2 hdld.	25.00
		Plate, 14″, hdld. torte	25.00
Mayonnaise set, 3 pc. scoop side bowl, spoon, tray	27.50	Plate, 14″, service	25.00
		Plate, 14″, torte	25.00
Mayonnaise set, 4 pc., plate, bowl, 2 ladles	35.00	Plate, 17″, cupped edge	35.00
		Plate, 17″, reg. edge	32.50
Mayonnaise w/7″ liner	22.50	Plate, 17″, torte	35.00
Mirror, 4″ rnd., standing	55.00	Plate w/indent, oval	10.00
Mustard jar w/spoon	30.00	Plate w/indent, 8″	12.50
Oil, 4 oz., bulbous bottom	32.50	Platter, 13″	45.00
Oil, 4 oz., hdld. bulbous bottom	40.00	Platter, 16″	77.50
Oil, 6 oz., hdld. bulbous bottom	40.00	Punch ladle	20.00
Oil, 6 oz., bulbous bottom	40.00	Punch set, family, 8 demi cups, ladle, lid	225.00
Oil w/stopper, etched "Oil"	45.00	Punch set, 15 pc. bowl on base, 12 cups, ladle	185.00
Oil w/stopper, etched "Vinegar"	45.00		
Oyster cocktail, #3400, 4 oz.	17.50	Relish & dressing set, 4 pc. (10½″ 4 pt. relish w/marmalade)	47.50
Party set, 2 pc., plate w/indent for cup	17.50	Salad fork & spoon set	17.50
Pitcher, 14 oz., short rnd.	65.00	Salad set, 4 pc., buffet; lg. rnd. tray, div. bowl, 2 spoons	60.00
Pitcher, 16 oz., low ft.	100.00		
Pitcher, 16 oz., no ice lip	75.00	Salad set, 4 pc. (rnd. plate, flared bowl, fork, spoon)	42.50
Pitcher, 20 oz.	85.00		
Pitcher, 40 oz., juice/cocktail	85.00	Salt & pepper, bead ft., straight side, chrome top	12.50
Pitcher, 40 oz., bead hdld. w/lip	100.00		
Pitcher, 64 oz.	97.50	Salt & pepper, bead ft., bulbous, chrome top	12.50
Pitcher, 80 oz.	125.00		
Plate, 4½″	4.00	Salt & pepper, bulbous w/bead stem, chrome top	10.00
Plate, 5½″, 2 hdld.	6.00		
Plate, 5½″, hdld.	7.50	Salt & pepper, pr., indiv.	6.00
Plate, 6″, bread/butter	6.50	Salt & pepper, pr., plastic top	8.00
Plate, 6″, canape w/off ctr. indent	7.50	Salt dip, 2″	5.50
Plate, 6¾″, 2 hdld. crimped	7.50	Salt dip, 2¼″	6.00
Plate, 7″, salad	8.00	Salt spoon, 3 bead hdld.	3.50
Plate, 7½″, 2 hdld.	7.50	Salt spoon w/ribbed bowl	3.50
Plate, 7½″, triangular	9.50	Sauce boat w/plate, set	75.00
Plate, 8″, oval	13.00	Saucer, after dinner	7.50
Plate, 8″, salad	8.00	Saucer, tea or coffee	3.00
Plate, 8¼″, crescent salad	22.50	Set: 2 pc. 14″ Chip plate w/div. dip bowl	47.50
Plate, 8½″, 2 hdld. crimped	12.50		
Plate, 8½″, 2 hdld.	12.00	Set: 2 pc. canape (plate w/indent; ftd. juice)	27.50
Plate, 8½″, salad	11.50		

CANDLEWICK, Line #400, Imperial Glass Company, 1936 - 1984 (continued)

	Crystal
Set: 2 pc. hdld. cracker w/cheese compote	42.50
Set: 2 pc. rnd. cracker plate w/indent; cheese compote	47.50
Snack jar w/cover, bead ft.	65.00
Snack jar w/cover, ftd.	77.50
Stem, #400, 1 oz., cordial, bead ft.	37.50
Stem, #400, 3 oz., cocktail, bead ft.	17.50
Stem, #400, 4 oz., cocktail, bead ft.	12.50
Stem, #400, 5 oz., juice tumbler, bead ft.	15.00
Stem, #400, 5 oz., tall sherbet, bead ft.	14.00
Stem, #400, 5 oz., wine, bead ft.	16.50
Stem, #400, 6 oz., sherbet	12.00
Stem, #400, 10 oz., bead ft.	13.00
Stem, #400, 11 oz., goblet	12.00
Stem, #400, 12 oz., tea	12.50
Stem, #3400, low sherbet	12.00
Stem, #3400, 1 oz., cordial, grad. bead	25.00
Stem, #3400, 4 oz., cocktail	17.00
Stem, #3400, 4 oz., wine	17.00
Stem, #3400, 5 oz., claret	17.50
Stem, #3400, 5 oz., ft. juice tumbler	17.50
Stem, #3400, 6 oz., parfait	17.00
Stem, #3400, 6 oz., sherbet/saucer champagne	16.00
Stem, #3400, 9 oz., goblet	16.00
Stem, #3800, low sherbet	12.00
Stem, #3800, brandy	17.50
Stem, #3800, cocktail	17.50
Stem, #3800, 1 oz. cordial	32.50
Stem, #3800, wine	18.00
Stem, #3800, goblet	17.50
Stem, #3800, claret	17.50
Stem, #3800, champagne/sherbet	15.00
Stem, #3800, 5 oz., juice tumbler	12.50
Stem, #3800, 6 oz., parfait	15.00
Stem, #3800, 9 oz., water	17.50
Stem, #3800, 12 oz., low ft. tea tumbler	18.00
Strawberry set, 2 pc. (7″ plate/sugar dip bowl)	15.00
Sugar, 6 oz., bead hdld.	6.50
Sugar, indiv. bridge	6.00
Sugar, plain ft.	6.50
Sugar/creamer w/6″ tray, set	20.00
Tete-a-tete 3 pc. brandy, a.d. cup, 6½″ oval tray	45.00
Tid bit server, 2 tier	40.00

	Crystal
Tid bit set, 3 pc. nest. heart	60.00
Toast w/cover, set	75.00
Tray, 2 hdld. crimped	27.50
Tray, 5½″, hdld.	12.50
Tray, 5½″, lemon, ctr. hdld.	13.50
Tray, 5¼″ x 9¼″, condiment	17.50
Tray, 5″	12.50
Tray, 6½″	15.00
Tray, 6″, wafer, handle bent to ctr. of dish	20.00
Tray, 7½″, hdld.	15.00
Tray, 8½″, hdld.	17.50
Tray, 10″, hdld.	22.50
Tray, 10½″, ctr. hdld. fruit	25.00
Tray, 11½″, ctr. hdld. party	30.00
Tray, 13½″, 2 hdld. celery	27.50
Tray, 13″, relish	27.50
Tray, 14″, hdld.	30.00
Tumbler, #400, 5 oz., bead ft. juice	10.00
Tumbler, #400, 7 oz., old fashioned	12.00
Tumbler, #400, 10 oz., bead ft.	12.00
Tumbler, #400, 12 oz., bead ft.	12.50
Tumbler, #400, 14 oz., bead ft. tea	16.00
Tumbler, #3400, 9 oz., ft.	14.00
Tumbler, #3400, 10 oz., plain ft.	12.00
Tumbler, #3800, 9 oz.	14.00
Tumbler, #3800, 12 oz.	17.50
Vase, 3¾″, ftd. ball	20.00
Vase, 4″, bead ft. sm. neck ball	17.50
Vase, 5¾″, bead ft. bud	22.50
Vase, 5¾″, bead ft. mini bud	22.50
Vase, 6″, flat, crimped edge	20.00
Vase, 6″, ftd. flared rim	22.00
Vase, 6″ diam.	75.00
Vase, 6½″ fan	25.00
Vase, 7″ ivy bowl	30.00
Vase, 7″ rolled rim w/bead hdld.	20.00
Vase, 7″ rose bowl	45.00
Vase, 7¼″ ftd. rose bowl, crimped	77.50
Vase, 7½″ ftd. rose bowl	67.50
Vase, 8″, fan w/bead hdld.	22.50
Vase, 8″, flat, crimped edge	25.00
Vase, 8″, fluted rim w/bead hdld.	27.50
Vase, 8¼″	25.00
Vase, 8½″, bead ft. bud	27.50
Vase, 8½″, bead ft., flared rim	22.00
Vase, 8½″, bead ft., inward rim	22.50
Vase, 8½″, hdld. (pitcher shape)	50.00
Vase, 10″, bead ft., straight side	45.00
Vase, 10″, ftd.	85.00

CAPE COD, Imperial Glass Co., 1932 - 1980's,

Colors: crystal, cobalt blue, red

What will happen to the moulds of this sister pattern of Candlewick is, also, very much up in the air at present. Prices on blue and red will be determined later.

See Page 3 For Last Minute Information!

	Crystal		Crystal
Ash tray, 4″, 160/134/1	5.00	Marmalade, 4 pc. set, 160/89	17.50
Ashtray, 5½″, 160/150	7.00	Mayonnaise, 3 pc. set, 160/52H	15.00
Basket, 9″, hdld., 160/221/0	30.00	Mayonnaise, 3 pc., 160/23	15.00
Basket, 11″, 160/40	40.00	Mustard, w/cover & spoon, 160/156	15.00
Bottle & stopper 26 oz., 160/244	25.00	Pitcher, milk, 1 pt., 160/240	20.00
Bowl, finger, 1602	5.00	Pitcher, ice lip, 2 qt., 160/239	25.00
Bowl, 3″, hdld. mint	7.00	Pitcher, blown, 5 pt., 160/176	30.00
Bowl, 4½″, 160/1W	4.00	Pitcher, 2 qt., 160/24	35.00
Bowl, 4½″, hdld. spider, 160/180	9.00	Pitcher, 48 oz., ftd., 16152	50.00
Bowl, 5″, dessert, heart shape, 160/49H	10.00	Plate, 6½″, bread & butter, 160/1D	3.00
Bowl, 5½″, fruit, 160/23B	6.00	Plate, 7″, 160/3D	5.00
Bowl, 5½″, hdld. spider, 160/181	12.00	Plate, 8″, center hdld. tray, 160/149D	12.50
Bowl, 6″, fruit, 160/3F	8.00	Plate, 8″, salad, 160/5D	8.00
Bowl, 6″, baked apple, 160/53X	8.00	Plate, 8½″, 2 hdld., 160/62D	10.00
Bowl, 6″, hdld., round mint, 160/51F	9.00	Plate, 8½″, hdld. server, 160/223	15.00
Bowl, 6″, hdld. heart, 160/40H	12.00	Plate, 9″, 160/7D	8.00
Bowl, 6″, hdld. mint, 160/51H	10.00	Plate, 10″, dinner, 160/10D	15.00
Bowl, 6″, hdld. tray, 160/51T	10.00	Plate, 11½″, 2 hdld., 160/145D	17.50
Bowl, 6½″, hdld. partioned spider, 160/187	12.00	Plate, 12″, multi server, 160/93	17.50
Bowl, 7½″, 160/7F	10.00	Plate, 14″, cupped, 160/75V	22.50
Bowl, 7½″, 2 hdld., 160/62B	12.00	Plate, 14″, salt, 160/75D	22.50
Bowl, 8¾″, 160/10F	12.50	Plate, 16″, cupped, 160/20V	25.00
Bowl, 9″, ftd. fruit, 160/67F	17.50	Relish, 9½″, 3 pt., 160/56	15.00
Bowl, 9½″, 2 hdld., 160/145B	15.00	Relish, 9½″, oval, 160/55	12.50
Bowl, 9½″, crimped, 160/221C	17.50	Relish, 11″, 5 part, 160/102	20.00
Bowl, 9½″, float, 160/221F	15.00	Salad set, 14″ plate, 12″ bowl, fork &	
Bowl, 10″, ftd., 160/137B	20.00	spoon, 160/75	65.00
Bowl, 12″, 160/75B	22.50	Salt & pepper, indiv., 160/251	4.00
Bowl, 12″, oval crimped, 160/131C	20.00	Salt & pepper, pr., ftd., 160/116	10.00
Bowl, 12″, punch, 160/20B	35.00	Salt & pepper, pr., 160/96	10.00
Butter, 5″, w/cover, hdld., 160/144	20.00	Salt dip, 160/61	4.00
Butter w/cover, ¼ lb., 160/161	15.00	Salt spoon, 1600	3.00
Cake stand, 10″, 4 toed, 160/220	20.00	Saucer, tea, 160/35	2.50
Cake stand, 10½″, ftd., 160/67D	30.00	Saucer, coffee, 160/37	3.00
Cake stand, 11″, 160/103D	40.00	Spoon, 160/701	5.00
Candleholder, twin, 160/100	15.00	Stem, 1½ oz., cordial, 1602	20.00
Candleholder, 3″, single, 160/170	10.00	Stem, 3 oz., wine, 1602	15.00
Candleholder, 4½″, saucer, 160/175	12.00	Stem, 3½ oz., cocktail, 1602	12.50
Candleholder, 5″, 160/80	12.50	Stem, 5 oz., claret, 1602	12.50
Candy w/cover, 160/110	20.00	Stem, 6 oz., low sundae, 1602	10.00
Celery, 8″, 160/105	12.00	Stem, 6 oz., parfait, 1602	15.00
Cigarette holder, ftd., 1602	9.00	Stem, 6 oz., sherbet, 1600	5.00
Coaster, w/spoon rest, 160/76	12.00	Stem, 6 oz., tall sherbet, 1602	11.00
Coaster, 3″, sq., 160/85	6.00	Stem, 9 oz., water, 1602	12.50
Coaster, 4″, 160/78	4.00	Stem, 10 oz., water, 1600	12.50
Comport, 6″, 160/45	12.00	Stem, 11 oz., dinner goblet, 1602	13.50
Comport, 6″, w/cover, ftd., 160/140	15.00	Stem, oyster cocktail, 1602	10.00
Comport, 7″, 160/48B	15.00	Sugar, 160/190	5.00
Creamer, 160/190	6.00	Sugar, 160/30	5.00
Creamer, 160/30	6.00	Sugar, ftd., 160/31	6.00
Creamer, ftd., 160/31	7.50	Tray, for creamer and sugar, 160/29	5.00
Cruet, w/stopper, 4 oz., 160/119	15.00	Tray, 7″, oblong, 160/29	8.00
Cruet, w/stopper, 5 oz., 160/70	35.00	Tray, 11″, pastry, 160/68D	15.00
Cup, tea, 160/35	5.00	Tumbler, 2½ oz., whiskey, 160	7.00
Cup, coffee, 160/37	7.50	Tumbler, 6 oz., ftd. juice, 1602	6.00
Cup, punch, 160/37	4.00	Tumbler, 6 oz., juice, 160	6.00
Decanter, bourbon, 160/260	30.00	Tumbler, 7 oz., old fashion, 160	8.00
Decanter, rye, 160/260	30.00	Tumbler, 10 oz., ftd. water, 1602	10.00
Decanter w/stopper, 160/163	35.00	Tumbler, 10 oz., water, 160	10.00
Decanter w/stopper, 24 oz., 160/212	35.00	Tumbler, 12 oz., ftd. iced tea, 1602	12.50
Egg cup, 160/225	10.00	Tumbler, 12 oz., ice tea, 160	12.50
Fork, 160/701	5.00	Tumbler, 14 oz., double old fashion, 160	12.50
Ladle, marmalade, 160/130	2.00	Tumbler, 16 oz., 160	15.00
Ladle, mayonnaise, 160/165	2.00	Vase, 6¼″, ftd., 160/22	15.00
Ladle, punch, 160/91	15.00	Vase, 10″, cylinder, 160/192	30.00
Marmalade, 3 pc. set, 160/89/3	15.00		

CAPRICE, Cambridge Glass Company, 1940's - Early 1950's

Colors: crystal, blue, white, amber, amethyst, pink, emerald green, pink, cobalt blue, moonlight blue, white

Yes, collectors, there is a punch bowl in Caprice. It was manufactured very late in Cambridge's history as was the quarter pound butter dish -- and only in crystal. I bought this one just a week before the photography session for this book. The candle reflectors shown are not very common and I have not heard of them in blue.

There have been some large price jumps since the last book, but especially noteworthy is the Doulton style pitcher. Any colors found will be priced near that of blue due to scarcity and lack of demand. Most colors are rare but there are fewer collectors.

See Page 3 For Last Minute Information!

	Crystal	Blue
Ash tray, 2¾", 3 ftd. shell	5.00	10.00
Ash tray, 3"	4.00	7.00
Ash tray, 4"	5.00	9.00
Ash tray, 5"	6.00	17.50
Bonbon, 6", oval, ftd.	15.00	27.50
Bonbon, 6" sq., 2 hdld.	10.00	20.00
Bonbon, 6" sq., ftd.	12.00	22.00
Bottle, 7 oz., bitters	50.00	125.00
Bowl, 5", 2 hdld., jelly	12.00	20.00
Bowl, 6½", hdld., 2 pt. relish	12.00	22.00
Bowl, 8", 4 ftd.	27.50	47.50
Bowl, 8", 3 pt. relish	17.50	27.50
Bowl, 9", crimped, 4 ftd.	27.50	49.50
Bowl, 9", pickle	12.50	25.00
Bowl, 10", salad, 4 ftd.	30.00	50.00
Bowl, 10", sq., 4 ftd.	30.00	50.00
Bowl, 10½", crimped, 4 ftd.	20.00	40.00
Bowl, 11", crimped, 4 ftd.	27.50	47.50
Bowl, 11", 2 hdld., oval, 4 ftd.	27.50	50.00
Bowl, 11¼", 4 pt. relish	29.50	52.50
Bowl, 12", relish, 3 pt.	30.00	75.00
Bowl, 12½", belled, 4 ftd.	27.50	47.50
Bowl, 12½", crimped, 4 ftd.	27.50	47.50
Bowl, 13", crimped, 4 ftd.	30.00	52.50
Bowl, 13½", 4 ftd., shallow belled	30.00	52.50
Bridge set:		
Cloverleaf, 6½"	20.00	37.50
Club, 6½"	20.00	37.50
Diamond, 6½"	20.00	37.50
Heart, 6½"	20.00	37.50
Spade, 6½"	20.00	37.50
Butterdish, ¼ lb.	195.00	----
Cake plate, 13" ftd.	125.00	250.00
Candle reflector	35.00	-----
Candlestick, 2½", ea.	11.50	17.50
Candlestick, 2-lite, keyhole, 5"	13.50	30.00
Candlestick, 3-lite	25.00	37.50
Candlestick, 5", ea., keyhole	12.00	25.00
Candlestick, 7", ea. w/prism	15.00	32.50
Candy, 6", 3 ftd. w/cover	35.00	72.50
Candy, 6", w/cover (divided or plain)	35.00	77.50
Celery & relish, 8½", 3 pt.	16.00	30.00
Cigarette box w/cover, 3½" x 2¼"	15.00	27.50
Cigarette box w/cover, 4½" x 3½"	17.50	32.50
Cigarette holder, 2" x 2¼", triangular	12.00	22.50
Cigarette holder, 3" x 3", triangular	13.50	32.50
Coaster, 3½"	12.00	20.00
Comport, 6"	15.50	32.50
Comport, 7" low ftd.	17.50	52.50
Comport, 7"	30.00	65.00
Cracker jar & cover	100.00	225.00
Creamer, 3 styles	10.00	15.00
Creamer, ind.	10.00	17.50
Cup	12.00	30.00
Decanter w/stopper, 35 oz.	75.00	145.00
Finger bowl & liner	25.00	45.00
Ice bucket	40.00	120.00
Marmalade w/cover, 6 oz.	37.50	85.00
Mayonnaise, 6½", 3 pc. set	22.50	47.50
Mayonnaise, 8", 3 pc. set	30.00	57.50

	Crystal	Blue
Mustard w/cover, 2 oz.	25.00	55.00
Oil, 3 oz., w/stopper	17.50	37.50
Oil, 5 oz., w/stopper	57.50	110.00
Pitcher, 32 oz., ball shape	45.00	265.00
Pitcher, 80 oz., ball shape	75.00	185.00
Pitcher, 90″, tall Doulton style	700.00	1,150.00
Plate, 6½″, bread/butter	6.00	12.50
Plate, 6½″, hdld., lemon	7.00	12.50
Plate, 7½″, salad	9.50	13.00
Plate, 8½″, luncheon	11.00	20.00
Plate, 9½″, dinner	32.50	90.00
Plate, 11″, cabaret, 4 ftd.	20.00	35.00
Plate, 11½″ cabaret	20.00	37.50
Plate, 14″ cabaret, 4 ftd.	27.50	45.00
Plate, 14″	25.00	45.00
Plate, 16″	30.00	55.00
Punch bowl, ftd.	1,000.00	----
Salad dressing, 3 pc., ftd. & hdld.	100.00	200.00
Saucer	2.50	5.00
Salt & pepper, pr., egg shape	30.00	60.00
Salt & pepper, pr., ball	27.50	50.00
Salt & pepper, pr., flat	20.00	----
Salt & pepper, indiv., ball, pr.	20.00	40.00
Salt & pepper, indiv., flat, pr.	18.00	----
Salver, 13″, 2 pc. (cake atop pedestal)	60.00	125.00
Stem, #300, blown, 1 oz. cordial	27.50	67.50
Stem, #300, blown, 2½ oz., wine	22.50	42.50
Stem, #300, blown, 3 oz., cocktail	20.00	35.00
Stem, #300, blown, 4½ oz., claret	22.50	42.50
Stem, #300, blown, 4½ oz., low oyster cocktail	12.00	22.50
Stem, #300, blown, 6 oz. sherbet	12.00	21.50
Stem, #300, blown, 9 oz. water	14.00	32.50
Stem, #301, blown, 1 oz., cordial	27.50	----
Stem, #301, blown, 2½ oz., wine	22.50	----
Stem, #301, blown, 3 oz., cocktail	20.00	----
Stem, #301, blown, 4½ oz., claret	22.50	----
Stem, #301, blown, 4½ oz., low oyster cocktail	10.00	----
Stem, #301, blown, 5 oz., juice	12.00	----
Stem, #301, blown, 6 oz., sherbet	12.00	----
Stem, #301, blown, 9 oz., water	15.00	----
Stem, #301, blown, 12 oz., tea	18.00	----
Stem, 3 oz., wine, molded	22.00	40.00
Stem, 3½ oz., cocktail, molded	22.00	37.50
Stem, 4½ oz., claret, molded	16.00	35.00
Stem, 4½ oz., fruit cocktail, molded	13.50	25.00
Stem, 5 oz., low sherbet, molded	15.00	22.50
Stem, 7 oz., tall sherbet, molded	17.50	30.00
Stem, 10 oz., water, molded	22.00	35.00
Sugar, sev. styles	10.00	15.00
Sugar, indiv.	10.00	15.00
Tray, for sugar & creamer	12.50	27.50
Tray, 6″ oval	12.00	20.00
Tumbler, 2 oz., flat, molded	10.00	20.00
Tumbler, 3 oz., ftd. molded	11.00	22.50
Tumbler, 5 oz., ftd., molded	14.00	22.50
Tumbler, 5 oz., flat, molded	15.00	25.00
Tumbler, #300, 5 oz., ftd. juice	15.00	25.00
Tumbler, 9 oz., straight side, molded	22.50	37.50
Tumbler, 10 oz., ftd., molded	17.50	32.50
Tumbler, 12 oz., ftd., molded	20.00	37.50
Tumbler, 12 oz., flat, molded	20.00	57.50
Tumbler, 12 oz., straight side, molded	25.00	42.50
Tumbler, #310, 12 oz., flat tea	27 50	52.50
Vase, 3½″	25.00	55.00
Vase, 4″, ivy bowl	25.00	55.00
Vase, 4½″	29.50	65.00
Vase, 5″, ivy bowl	35.00	67.50
Vase, 5½″	35.00	67.50
Vase, 6″	40.00	72.50
Vase, 6″, rose bowl	40.00	72.50
Vase, 6½″	45.00	77.50
Vase, 7½″	40.00	82.50
Vase, 8″, rose bowl	45.00	97.50
Vase, 8½″	50.00	107.50
Vase, 9½″	60.00	135.00

CARIBBEAN, Line #112, Duncan Miller Glass Company, 1936 - 1955

Colors: blue, crystal, amber, red

Blue is the color predominantly collected in this pattern. You will find a few pieces in amber and red priced in the range of the blue. Many crystal pieces will have applied, colored handles.

There may be items not listed; so let me hear from you about what you find.

	Blue
Ash tray, 6″, 4 indent.	25.00
Bowl, 3¾″ x 5″, folded side, hdld.	20.00
Bowl, 4½″ finger	15.00
Bowl, 5″, fruit nappy (takes liner), hdld.	12.00
Bowl, 5″ x 7″, folded side, hdld.	22.00
Bowl, 6½″, soup (takes liner)	20.00
Bowl, 7″, hdld.	25.00
Bowl, 7¼″, ftd., hdld. grapefruit	22.00
Bowl, 8½″	35.00
Bowl, 9″, salad	40.00
Bowl, 9¼″, veg., flared edge	30.00
Bowl, 9¼″, veg., hdld.	30.00
Bowl, 9½″, epergne, flared edge	35.00
Bowl, 10″, 6¼ qt. punch	90.00
Bowl, 10″, 6¼ qt. punch, flared top	95.00
Bowl, 10¾″, oval flower, hdld.	35.00
Bowl, 12″, console, flared edge	40.00
Candelabrum, 4¾″, 2-lite	40.00
Candlestick, 7¼″, 1-lite, w/bl. prisms	65.00
Candy dish w/cover, 4″ x 7″	50.00
Cheese/cracker, compote, 3½″ h., plate 11″, hdld.	45.00
Cigarette holder, (stack ashtray top)	50.00
Cocktail shaker, 9″, 33 oz.	100.00
Creamer	12.50
Cruet	47.50
Cup, tea	25.50
Cup, punch	10.00
Epergne, 4 pt., flower (12″ bowl; 9½″ bowl; 7¾″ vase, 14″ plate)	150.00
Ice bucket, 6½″, hdld.	75.00
Ladle, punch	50.00
Mayonnaise w/liner, 5¾″, 2 pt., 2 spoons, hdld.	45.00
Mayonnaise w/liner, 5¾″, hdld., 1 spoon	40.00
Mustard, 4″, w/slotted cover	55.00
Pitcher, 4¼″, 9 oz., syrup	65.00
Pitcher, 4¾″, 16 oz., milk	75.00
Pitcher w/ice lip, 9″, 72 oz., water	185.00
Plate, 6″, hdld. fruit nappy liner	8.00
Plate, 6¼″, bread/butter	6.00
Plate, 7¼″, rolled edge soup liner	10.00
Plate, 7½″, salad	14.00
Plate, 8″, hdld. mayonnaise liner	10.00
Plate, 8½″, luncheon	17.50
Plate, 10½″, dinner	60.00
Plate, 11″, hdld. cheese/cracker liner	30.00
Plate, 12″, salad liner, rolled edge	30.00
Plate, 16″, torte	40.00
Plate, 18″, punch underliner	50.00
Relish, 6″, round, 2 pt.	15.00

	Blue
Relish, 9½″, 4 pt., oblong	40.00
Relish, 9½″, oblong	40.00
Relish, 12¾″, 5 pt., rnd.	45.00
Relish, 12¾″, 7 pt., rnd.	45.00
Salt dip, 2½″	9.00
Salt & pepper, 3″, metal tops	40.00
Salt & pepper, 5″, metal tops	50.00
Saucer	5.00
Server, 5¾″, ctr. hdld.	35.00
Server, 6½″, ctr. hdld.	40.00
Stem, 3″, 1 oz., cordial	75.00
Stem, 3½″, 3½ oz., ftd., ball stem wine	25.00
Stem, 3⅝″, 2½ oz., wine (egg cup shape)	25.00
Stem, 4″, 6 oz., ftd., ball stem champagne	20.00
Stem, 4¼″, ftd. sherbet	12.50
Stem, 4¾″, 3 oz., ftd. ball stem wine	35.00
Stem, 5¾″, 8 oz., ftd., ball stem	25.00
Sugar	12.00
Tray, 6¼″, hand., mint, div.	15.00
Tray, 12¾″, rnd.	28.00
Tumbler, 2¼″, 2 oz., shot glass	35.00
Tumbler, 3½″, 5 oz. flat	17.50
Tumbler, 5¼″, 11½ oz., flat	22.50
Tumbler, 5½″, 8½ oz., ftd.	25.00
Tumbler, 6½″, 11 oz., ftd. iced tea	27.50
Vase, 5¾″, ftd., ruffled edge	20.00
Vase, 7¼″, ftd., flared edge, ball	25.00
Vase, 7½″, ftd., flared edge, bulbous	27.50
Vase, 7¾″, flared edge epergne	30.00
Vase, 8″, ftd., straight side	35.00
Vase, 9″, ftd., ruffled top	40.00
Vase, 10″, ftd.	40.00

CHANTILLY, Cambridge Glass Company, late 1940's - Early 1950's

Colors: crystal

Who was it, the "Big Bopper", who sang of "Chantilly lace and a pretty face" in the rock 'n roll tune of the late 1950's?

Chantilly lace was very popular among the brides of this era; no doubt, Cambridge was cognizant of that when they produced this pattern, though strictly speaking, the exquisite lace of Chantilly, France, was black rather than white bridal lace.

Some collectors have trouble distinguishing between Chantilly and Elaine, another Cambridge pattern.

	Crystal		Crystal
Bowl, 7", bonbon, 2 hdld. ftd.	15.00	Stem, #3600, 4½ oz., low oyster cocktail	15.00
Bowl, 7", relish/pickle, 2 pt.	17.50	Stem, #3600, 7 oz. tall sherbet	17.50
Bowl, 7", relish or pickle	17.50	Stem, #3600, 7 oz., low sherbet	15.00
Bowl, 9", celery/relish, 3 pt.	20.00	Stem, #3600, 10 oz., water	19.50
Bowl, 10", 4 ftd. flared	25.00	Stem, #3625, 1 oz., cordial	39.50
Bowl, 11", tab hdld.	22.50	Stem, #3625, 3 oz., cocktail	24.00
Bowl, 11½", tab hdld. ftd.	27.50	Stem, #3625, 4½ oz. claret	22.50
Bowl, 12", celery/relish, 3 pt.	27.50	Stem, #3625, 4½ oz., low oyster cocktail	15.00
Bowl, 12", 4 ftd. flared	27.50	Stem, #3625, 7 oz., low sherbet	15.00
Bowl, 12", 4 ftd. oval	32.50	Stem, #3625, 7 oz., tall sherbet	17.50
Bowl, 12", celery/relish, 5 pt.	29.50	Stem, #3625, 10 oz., water	22.50
Butter w/cover	135.00	Stem, #3775, 1 oz., cordial	39.50
Candlestick, 5"	17.50	Stem, #3775, 2½ oz., wine	25.00
Candlestick, 6", 2-lite, "fleur de lis"	26.00	Stem, #3775, 3 oz., cocktail	25.00
Candlestick, 6", 3-lite	30.00	Stem, #3775, 4½ oz., claret	22.50
Candy box w/cover, ftd.	110.00	Stem, #3775, 4½ oz., oyster cocktail	15.00
Candy box w/cover, rnd.	50.00	Stem, #3775, 6 oz., low sherbet	15.00
Cocktail icer, 2 pc.	30.00	Stem, #3775, 6 oz., tall sherbet	17.50
Comport, 5½"	30.00	Stem, #3779, 1 oz., cordial	45.00
Comport, 5⅜", blown	35.00	Stem, #3779, 2½ oz., wine	27.50
Creamer	13.50	Stem, #3779, 3 oz., cocktail	25.00
Creamer, indiv. #3900 scalloped edge	11.00	Stem, #3779, 4½ oz., claret	25.00
Cup	12.50	Stem, #3779, 4½ oz., low oyster cocktail	15.00
Decanter, ftd.	135.00	Stem, #3779, 6 oz. tall sherbet	17.50
Hurricane lamp, candlestick base	75.00	Stem, #3779, 6 oz. low sherbet	15.00
Hurricane lamp, keyhole base w/prisms	90.00	Stem, #3779, 9 oz., water	20.00
Ice bucket w/chrome handle	60.00	Sugar	13.50
Mayonnaise, (sherbet type bowl w/ladle)	25.00	Sugar, indiv. #3900, scalloped edge	11.00
Mayonnaise div. w/liner & 2 ladles	35.00	Tumbler, #3600, 5 oz., ftd. juice	14.00
Mayonnaise w/liner & ladle	30.00	Tumbler, #3600, 12 oz., ftd. tea	18.00
Oil, 6 oz., hdld. w/stopper	42.50	Tumbler, #3625, 5 oz., ftd. juice	13.50
Pitcher, ball	110.00	Tumbler, #3625, 10 oz., ftd. water	15.00
Pitcher, Doulton	185.00	Tumbler, #3625, 12 oz., ftd tea	18 00
Pitcher, upright	150.00	Tumbler, #3775, 5 oz., ftd. juice	14.00
Plate, 6½", bread/butter	6.50	Tumbler, #3775, 10 oz., ftd. water	15.00
Plate, 8", salad	12.50	Tumbler, #3775, 12 oz., ftd. tea	17.50
Plate, 8", tab hdld., ftd. bonbon	15.00	Tumbler, #3779, 5 oz., ftd. juice	14.00
Plate, 10½", dinner	40.00	Tumbler, #3779, 12 oz., ftd. tea	18.00
Plate, 12", 4 ftd. service	22.50	Tumbler, 13 oz.	20.00
Plate, 13", 4 ftd.	30.00	Vase, 5", globe	26.00
Plate, 13½", tab hdld. cake	30.00	Vase, 6", high ftd. flower	18.00
Plate, 14", torte	30.00	Vase, 8", high ftd. flower	22.00
Salt & pepper, pr.	27.50	Vase, 9", keyhole base	27.50
Saucer	2.50	Vase, 10", bud	22.00
Stem, #3600, 1 oz., cordial	39.50	Vase, 11", ftd. flower	35.00
Stem, #3600, 2½ oz., cocktail	24.00	Vase, 11", ped. ftd. flower	37.50
Stem, #3600, 2½ oz., wine	27.50	Vase, 12", keyhole base	35.00
Stem, #3600, 4½ oz., claret	22.50	Vase, 13", ftd. flower	45.00

Note: See Pages 148-149 for stem identification.

CHEROKEE ROSE, Tiffin Glass Company, 1940's - 1950's

Colors: crystal

Cherokee Rose rivaled Cambridge's "Rose Point" and Heisey's "Orchid" pattern as bridal giftware in the late 1940's. In fact, the lady who sold me the pieces you see here said she'd had it since 1948.

Notice the beading on the pieces which is reminiscent of Heisey's "Waverly" blank. If you think of the Cherokee Rose design as being THREE cameo's, you're less likely to confuse it with "Rose Point" which is a single cameo design with roses within. Or, you may prefer to remember this as the cameo with the urn inside. However, it's a beautiful pattern that is coming to the attention of collectors, particularly those who have moved from Depression Glass per se into collecting the better glasswares of the time.

Most Tiffin patterns seem to have a multitude of stems. Both the wine and the cocktail hold 3½ ounces. The wine is pictured on the left while the cocktail is on the right side.

I doubt this listing is complete. Please let me hear of your finds in Cherokee Rose!

	Crystal		Crystal
Bowl, 5", finger	10.00	Stem, 2 oz., sherry	17.50
Bowl, 6", fruit or nut	12.00	Stem, 3½ oz. cocktail	15.00
Bowl, 7", salad	15.00	Stem, 3½ oz., wine	25.00
Bowl, 10", deep salad	22.50	Stem, 4 oz., claret	22.50
Bowl, 10½", celery, oblong	20.00	Stem, 4½ oz. parfait	20.00
Bowl, 12", crimped	25.00	Stem, 5½ oz., sherbet/champagne	12.50
Bowl, 12½", centerpiece, flared	27.50	Stem, 9 oz., water	20.00
Bowl, 13", centerpiece	30.00	Sugar	10.00
Cake plate, 12½", center hdld.	27.50	Table bell	35.00
Candlesticks, pr. double branch	40.00	Tumbler, 4½ oz., oyster cocktail	11.00
Comport, 6"	17.50	Tumbler, 5 oz., ftd. juice	12.50
Creamer	11.50	Tumbler, 8 oz., ftd. water	15.00
Mayonnaise, liner and ladle	32.50	Tumbler, 10½ oz., ftd. iced tea	17.50
Pitcher	100.00	Vase, 6", bud	15.00
Plate, 6", sherbet	4.50	Vase, 8", bud	20.00
Plate, 8", luncheon	9.50	Vase, 8½", tear drop	27.50
Plate, 13½", turned-up edge, lily	32.50	Vase, 9¼", tub	35.00
Plate, 14", sandwich	20.00	Vase, 10", bud	25.00
Relish, 6½", 3 part	17.50	Vase, 11", bud	30.00
Relish, 12½", 3 pt.	25.00	Vase, 11", urn	32.50
Stem, 1 oz., cordial	40.00	Vase, 12" flared	40.00

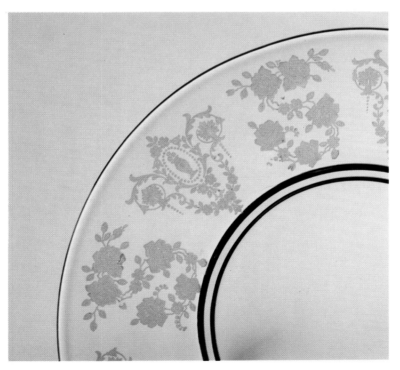

CHINTZ, #1401 (Empress Blank) and CHINTZ #3389 (Duquesne Blank) A.H. Heisey Co., 1931-1938

Colors: crystal; "Sahara" yellow; "Moongleam" green; "Flamingo" pink, and "Alexandrite" orchid

	Crystal	Sahara
Bowl, finger, #4107	8.00	15.00
Bowl, 5½", ftd. preserve, hdld.	15.00	27.00
Bowl, 6", ftd. mint	18.00	30.00
Bowl, 6", ftd., 2 hdld, jelly	15.00	30.00
Bowl, 7", triplex relish	16.00	30.00
Bowl, 7½", Nasturtium	16.00	30.00
Bowl, 8½", ftd., 2 hdld. floral	32.00	65.00
Bowl, 11", dolp. ft. floral	35.00	75.00
Bowl, 13", 2 pt., pickle & olive	15.00	25.00
Comport, 7", oval	35.00	70.00
Creamer, 3 dolp. ftd.	20.00	42.50
Grapefruit, ftd. #3389, Duquesne	22.00	40.00
Ice bucket, ftd.	60.00	100.00
Mayonnaise, 5½", dolp. ft.	35.00	65.00
Oil, 4 oz.	35.00	100.00
Pitcher, 3 pint, dolp. ft.	75.00	175.00
Plate, 6", square bread	6.00	15.00
Plate, 7", square salad	8.00	18.00
Plate, 8", square luncheon	10.00	22.00
Plate, 10½", square dinner	25.00	60.00
Platter, 14", oval	25.00	45.00
Stem, #3389, Duquesne, 1 oz., cordial	80.00	150.00
Stem, #3389, 2½ oz., wine	17.50	42.50
Stem, #3389, 3 oz., cocktail	15.00	35.00
Stem, #3389, 4 oz., claret	17.50	40.00
Stem, #3389, 4 oz., oyster cocktail	10.00	20.00
Stem, #3389, 5 oz., parfait	12.00	25.00
Stem, #3389, 5 oz., saucer champagne	11.00	22.50
Stem, #3389, 5 oz., sherbet	8.00	17.50
Stem, #3389, 9 oz., water	15.00	30.00
Sugar, 3 dolp. ft.	20.00	42.50
Tray, 10", celery	14.00	27.50
Tray, 12", sq., ctr. hdld. sandwich	35.00	65.00
Tray, 13", celery	18.00	26.00
Tumbler, #3389, 5 oz., ftd. juice	11.00	22.00
Tumbler, #3389, 8 oz., soda	12.00	24.00
Tumbler, #3389, 10 oz., ftd. water	13.00	25.00
Tumbler, #3389, 12 ., iced tea	14.00	27.50
Vase, 9"dolp. ft.	65.00	125.00

CLEO, Cambridge Glass Company, Introduced 1930

Colors: amber, blue, crystal, green, pink, yellow

In the time since the first Elegant book, I have found more unusual pieces in Cleo than in any other pattern in this book. The most interesting is shown on the next page in the center, a handled, three-part relish. If you look closely, you will see the Cleo etching on the bottom, but Apple Blossom is etched completely around the outside edge. The tobacco humidor is the first to show up with a major etching and only a few of the miniature console bowls have appeared. Now I am trying to figure out what the amber piece in the foreground goes with as I found it with a small console; but upon closer inspection, it is made to go upside down from the way it is pictured. Any ideas?

I am sure that my listing for Cleo is only in its infancy; the more I find, the more that seems not to be listed in old catalogs. Remember that if you have items not listed, send me the information; a photo for verification helps. It has taken over a dozen years to get Depression Glass listings about 99% correct; it will probably take even longer with the handmade glass.

In the list below, amber and crystal will sell a little under the prices listed except in unusual pieces; the blue will exceed prices listed by 20%.

	All Colors
Basket, 7″, 2 hdld. (upturned sides) DECAGON	17.50
Basket, 11″, 2 hdld. (upturned sides) DECAGON	30.00
Bouillon cup w/saucer, 2 hdld. DECAGON ..	22.50
Bowl, 2 pt. relish	19.50
Bowl, 5½″, fruit	12.50
Bowl, 5½″, 2 hdld., bonbon DECAGON.....	17.50
Bowl, 6″, 4 ft., comport	30.00
Bowl, 6″, cereal, DECAGON	15.00
Bowl, 6½″, 2 hdld., bonbon DECAGON.....	20.00
Bowl, 6½″, cranberry	15.00
Bowl, 7½″, tab hdld. soup	25.00
Bowl, 8″, miniature console	85.00
Bowl, 8½″	30.00
Bowl, 8½″, 2 hdld. DECAGON	32.50
Bowl, 9″, covered vegetable	75.00
Bowl, 9½″, oval veg., DECAGON	32.50
Bowl, 9″, pickle, DECAGON	17.50
Bowl, 10″, 2 hdld DECAGON	20.00
Bowl, 11″, oval	25.00
Bowl, 11½″, oval	27.50
Bowl, 12″, console	32.50
Bowl, cream soup w/saucer, 2 hdld. DECAGON	25.00
Bowl, finger w/liner #3077	22.00
Bowl, finger w/liner #3115	22.00
Candlestick, 1-lite, 2 styles	22.50
Candlestick, 2-lite	32.50
Candy box	57.50
Comport, 7″, tall #3115	35.00
Creamer, DECAGON	17.50
Creamer, ftd.	15.00
Cup, DECAGON	15.00
Decanter and stopper	75.00
Gravy boat w/liner plate DECAGON........	67.50
Ice pail	57.50
Ice tub	42.50
Mayonnaise w/liner and ladle, DECAGON ..	39.50
Mayonnaise, ftd.	25.00
Oil, 6 oz., w/stopper DECAGON	65.00
Pitcher, 3½ pt. #38	125.00
Pitcher w/cover, 22 oz.	100.00
Pitcher w/cover 60 oz., #804	175.00

	All Colors
Pitcher w/cover, 62 oz. #955	185.00
Pitcher w/cover, 63 oz. #3077	175.00
Pitcher w/cover, 68 oz. #937	195.00
Plate, 7″	11.50
Plate, 7″, 2 hdld DECAGON...............	13.50
Plate, 9½″, dinner DECAGON	35.00
Plate, 11″, 2 hdld. DECAGON	22.50
Platter, 12″	32.50
Platter, 15″	47.50
Platter w/cover	125.00
Platter, indented w/sauce & spoon	250.00
Saucer, DECAGON	3.00
Server, 12″, ctr. hand.	35.00
Stem, #3077, 1 oz., cordial	72.50
Stem, #3077, 2½ oz., cocktail	25.00
Stem, #3077, 3½ oz. wine	52.50
Stem, #3077, 6 oz, low sherbet...........	12.50
Stem, #3077, 6 oz., tall sherbet...........	15.00
Stem, #3115, 9 oz.	25.00
Stem, #3115, 3½ oz., cocktail	25.00
Stem, #3115, 6 oz., fruit	12.50
Stem, #3115, 6 oz., low sherbet	12.50
Stem, #3115, 6 oz., tall sherbet...........	15.00
Stem, #3115, 9 oz.	25.00
Sugar, DECAGON	17.50
Sugar, ftd.	15.00
Tobacco humidor	250.00
Tray, 12″, oval service DECAGON	25.00
Tumbler, #3077, 2½ oz., ftd.	17.50
Tumbler, #3077 5 oz., ftd.	16.50
Tumbler, #3077, 8 oz., ftd.	20.00
Tumbler, #3077, 10 oz., ftd.	22.50
Tumbler, #3077, 12 oz., ftd.	25.00
Tumbler, #3115, 2½ oz., ftd.	19.50
Tumbler, #3115, 5 oz., ftd.	17.50
Tumbler, #3115, 8 oz., ftd.	20.00
Tumbler, #3115, 10 oz., ftd.	22.50
Tumbler, #3115, 12 oz., ftd.	25.00
Tumbler, 12 oz., flat.	27.50
Vase, 5½″	47.50
Vase, 9½″	77.50
Vase, 11″	97.50

COLONY, Line #2412, Fostoria Glass Company, 1920's - 1980's

Colors: crystal; some blue, green, yellow, white, red 1980's

This Fostoria pattern was extremely popular in the 1950's and many people who got it for wedding gifts are beginning to search for replacement pieces. This is how many new collectors are introduced to glass collecting and to glass shows in particular. Some promoters are beginning to advertise shows as a glass matching service.

	Crystal
Bowl, ftd. almond	4.50
Bowl, 4½", rnd.	5.50
Bowl, 4¾", finger	7.00
Bowl, 5", rnd.	6.00
Bowl, 5½", sq.	5.50
Bowl, 5¾", high ft.	8.50
Bowl, 7", olive, oblong	8.00
Bowl, 8", hdld.	10.00
Bowl, 9", low ft.	15.00
Bowl, 9", high ft.	15.00
Bowl, 9½", pickle	12.00
Bowl, 10½", low ft.	22.00
Bowl, 10½", high ft.	25.00
Bowl, 11½", celery	12.50
Candlestick, 3½"	8.00
Candlestick, 7½", w/8 prisms	25.00
Candlestick, 9¾"	14.00
Candlestick, 14½", w/10 prisms	35.00
Candy w/cover, 6½"	25.00
Cheese compote w/cracker plate	24.50
Cream soup, ftd.	8.00
Creamer, indiv.	8.00
Creamer, 3¾"	9.00
Comport, 4"	11.00
Cup, ftd.	5.00
Stem, 3⅜", oyster cocktail, 4 oz.	9.00
Stem, 3⅝", sherbet, 5 oz.	10.00
Stem, 4¼", wine, 3¼ oz.	15.00
Stem, 4", cocktail, 3½ oz.	10.00
Stem, 5¼", goblet, 9 oz.	15.00
Mayonnaise w/liner	15.00
Oil w/stopper	27.50
Pitcher, ftd., milk	35.00
Pitcher, 64 oz.	40.00
Plate, ctr. hdld. sand.	22.50
Plate, 6"	2.50
Plate, 7"	3.00
Plate, 8"	3.50
Plate, 9"	4.50
Plate, 10"	12.50
Plate, 12", ftd. salver	20.00
Plate, 13", torte	17.50
Salt, indiv.	5.50
Salt & pepper, pr.	12.50
Saucer	1.50
Sugar, indiv.	5.00
Sugar, 3½"	7.50
Tray for indiv. sugar/creamer	7.00
Tumbler, 5 oz.	8.00
Tumbler, 9 oz.	10.00
Tumbler, 4½", 5 oz., ftd.	10.50
Tumbler, 5¾", 12 oz. ftd.	12.00
Tumbler, 12 oz.	13.00
Vase, 8"	25.00

CRYSTOLITE, Blank #1503, A. H. Heisey & Co.

Colors: crystal, Zircon/Limelight, Sahara and rare in amber

	Crystal
Ash tray, 3½", square	4.00
Ash tray, 4½", square	4.50
Ash tray, 5", w/book match	25.00
Ash tray (coaster), 4", rnd.	5.00
Basket, 6", hdld.	350.00
Bonbon, 7", shell	17.00
Bonbon, 7½", 2 hdld.	15.00
Bottle, 1 qt. rye, #107 stopper	150.00
Bottle, 4 oz. bitters w/short tube	75.00
Bottle, 4 oz. cologne w/#108 stopper	60.00
w/drip stop	145.00
Bottle, syrup w/drip & cut top	55.00
Bowl, 7½ quart punch	90.00
Bowl, 2", indiv. swan nut (or ash tray)	15.00
Bowl, 3", indiv. nut, hdld.	15.00
Bowl, 4½", dessert (or nappy)	6.00
Bowl, 5", preserve	12.00
Bowl, 5", thousand island dressing, ruffled top	16.00
Bowl, 5½", dessert	8.00
Bowl, 6", oval jelly, 4 ft.	13.00
Bowl, 6", preserve, 2 hdld.	13.00
Bowl, 7", shell praline	25.00
Bowl, 8", dessert (sauce)	15.00
Bowl, 8", 2 pt. conserve, hdld.	16.00
Bowl, 9", leaf pickle	17.00
Bowl, 10", salad, rnd.	23.00
Bowl, 11", w/attached mayonnaise (chip 'n dip)	55.00
Bowl, 12", gardenia, shallow	30.00
Bowl, 13", oval floral, deep	30.00
Candle block, 1-lite, sq.	12.00
Candle block, 1-lite, swirl	12.00
Candlestick, 1-lite, ftd.	12.00
Candlestick, 1-lite, w/#4233 5", vase	25.00
Candlestick, 2-lite	20.00
Candlestick, 2-lite, bobeche & 10 "D" prisms	50.00
Candlestick sans vase, 3-lite	17.00
Candlestick w/#4233 5", vase, 3-lite	30.00
Candy, 6½", swan	35.00
Candy box w/cover, 5½"	45.00
Candy box w/cover, 7"	50.00
Cheese, 5½", ftd.	9.00
Cigarette box w/cover, 4"	15.00
Cigarette box w/cover, 4½"	17.00
Cigarette holder, ftd.	17.50
Cigarette holder, oval	12.00
Cigarette holder, rnd.	10.00
Cigarette lighter	10.00
Coaster, 4"	6.00
Cocktail shaker, 1 qt. w/#1 strainer; #86 stopper	125.00
Comport, 5", ftd., deep	25.00
Creamer, indiv.	12.00
Cup	10.00
Cup, punch or custard	8.00
Hurricane block, 1-lite, sq.	25.00
Hurricane block w/#4061, 10" plain globe, 1-lite, sq.	50.00
Ice tub w/silver plate handle	75.00
Jam jar w/cover	45.00
Ladle, glass, punch	25.00
Ladle, plastic	7.50
Mayonnaise, 5½", shell, 3 ft.	30.00
Mayonnaise, 6", oval, hdld.	20.00
Mayonnaise ladle	7.00
Mustard & cover	35.00
Oil bottle, 3 oz.	35.00
Oil bottle w/stopper, 2 oz.	25.00
Oval creamer, sugar w/tray, set	45.00
Pitcher, ½ gallon, ice, blown	65.00
Pitcher, 2 quart swan, ice lip	750.00
Plate, 7", salad	8.00
Plate, 7", shell	12.00
Plate, 7", underliner for 1000 island dressing bowl	7.00
Plate, 7½", coupe	30.00
Plate, 8", oval, mayonnaise liner	9.00
Plate, 8½", salad	15.00
Plate, 10½", service	50.00
Plate, 11", ftd. cake salver	250.00
Plate, 11", torte	24.00
Plate, 12", sand.	24.00
Plate, 14", sand.	27.50
Plate, 14", torte	27.50
Plate, 20", buffet or punch liner	40.00
Puff box w/cover, 4¾"	50.00
Salad dressing set, 3 pc.	35.00
Salt & pepper, pr.	30.00
Saucer	5.00
Stem, 1 oz., cordial, wide optic, blown	75.00
Stem, 3½ oz., cocktail, w.o., blown	20.00
Stem, 3½ oz., claret, w.o., blown	25.00
Stem, 3½ oz., oyster cocktail, w.o. blown	20.00
Stem, 6 oz., sherbet/saucer champagne	12.00
Stem, 10 oz., w.o., blown	17.50
Sugar, indiv.	12.00
Tray, 5½", oval, liner indiv. creamer/sugar	35.00
Tray, 9", 4 pt. leaf relish	22.50
Tray, 10", 5 pt., rnd. relish	35.00
Tray, 12", 3 pt. relish	25.00
Tray, 12", rect., celery	35.00
Tray, 12", rect., celery/olive	35.00
Tumbler, 5 oz., ftd., juice, w.o., blown	15.00
Tumbler, 10 oz., pressed	15.00
Tumbler, 10 oz., iced tea, w.o., blown	20.00
Tumbler, 12 oz., ftd., iced tea, w.o., blown	18.00
Urn, 7", flower	17.50
Vase, 3", short stem	17.50
Vase, 6", ftd.	17.50

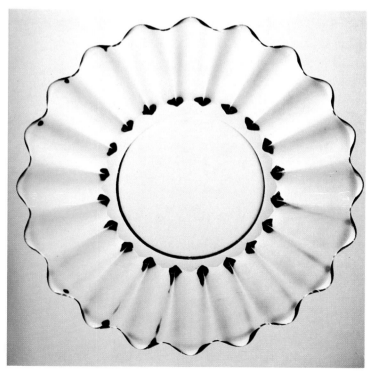

"CUPID", Paden City Glass Company, 1930's

Colors: pink, green, light blue, black

	Pink, Blue, Green
Bowl, 8½", oval, ftd.	30.00
Bowl, 9¼", fruit, ftd.	27.50
Bowl, 9¼", ctr. hdld.	32.50
Bowl, 11", console	32.50
Cake, 11¾"	35.00
Candlestick, 5" wide	17.50
Candy w/lid, ftd., 4¾", high	37.50
Candy w/lid, 3 pt.	47.50
Comport, 6¼"	20.00
Creamer, 4½", ftd.	25.00
Creamer, 5", ftd.	32.50
Ice bucket, 6"	47.50
Ice tub, 4¾"	38.50
Mayonnaise, 6"diam./fits 8" plate	37.50
Plate, 8"	15.00
Plate, 10½"	25.00
Sugar, 4¼", ftd.	25.00
Sugar, 5", ftd.	32.50
Tray, 10½", ctr. hdld.	27.50
Tray, 10⅞", oval, ftd.	35.00
Vase, 8¼", elliptical	57.50

DANCING GIRL, Morgantown Glass Works, Early 1930's

Colors: pink, green, blue

	All Colors
Creamer	30.00
Pitcher	150.00
Plate, 5⅞", sherbet	7.50
Plate, 7½"	15.00
Stem, 2½", 3½ oz., oyster cocktail	20.00
Stem, 4¾", 7 oz., sherbet	25.00
Stem, 7¾", 9 oz. banquet wine	35.00
Sugar	27.50
Tumbler, 4¾", 9 oz.	25.00
Tumbler, 5½", 11 oz.	30.00
Vase, 10", slender bud	35.00

DECAGON, Cambridge Glass Company, 1930's

Colors: green, pink, red, cobalt blue, amber, Moonlight blue

The stemware pictured has etched patterns. It was easier and cheaper to use what I already had (for other pictures) on Decagon blanks than to go buy plain Decagon. That blue relish is missing an insert due to clumsy handling; so if anyone out there has a spare, let me know.

	Pastel Colors	Red Blue
Basket, 7″, 2 hdld. (upturned sides)	12.00	20.00
Bowl, bouillon w/liner	7.50	12.50
Bowl, cream soup w/liner	10.00	22.00
Bowl, 2½″, indiv. almond	15.00	25.00
Bowl, 3¾″, flat rim cranberry	10.00	14.00
Bowl, 3½″, belled cranberry	9.00	14.00
Bowl, 5½″, 2 hdld. bonbon	10.00	17.00
Bowl, 5½″, belled fruit	5.50	10.00
Bowl, 5¾″, flat rim fruit	6.00	11.00
Bowl, 6″, belled cereal	7.00	12.50
Bowl, 6″, flat rim cereal	6.00	11.00
Bowl, 6″, ftd. almond	20.00	35.00
Bowl, 6¼″, 2 hdld., bonbon	10.00	17.00
Bowl, 8½″, flat rim soup "plate"	8.00	15.00
Bowl, 9″, rnd. veg.	14.00	24.00
Bowl, 9″, 2 pt. relish	9.00	15.00
Bowl, 9½″, oval veg.	12.00	22.00
Bowl, 10″, berry	10.00	17.50
Bowl, 10½″, oval veg.	16.00	27.50
Bowl, 11″, rnd. veg.	16.00	30.00
Bowl, 11″, 2 pt. relish	10.00	17.50
Comport, 5¾″	12.50	20.00
Comport, 6½″, low ft.	15.00	25.00
Comport, 7″, tall	17.50	27.50
Creamer, ftd.	9.00	20.00
Creamer, scalloped edge	8.00	18.00
Creamer, lightning bolt handles	7.00	12.00
Creamer, tall, lg. ft.	10.00	22.00
Cup	6.00	10.00
French dressing bottle, "Oil/Vinegar"	40.00	65.00
Gravy boat w/2 hdld. liner (like spouted cream soup)	55.00	85.00
Mayonnaise, 2 hdld. w/2 hdld. liner and ladle	20.00	35.00
Mayonnaise w/liner & ladle	18.00	30.00
Oil, 6 oz., tall, w/hdld. & stopper	40.00	65.00
Plate, 6¼″, bread/butter	3.00	5.00
Plate, 7″, 2 hdld.	9.00	15.00
Plate, 7½″	4.00	10.00
Plate, 8½″, salad	6.00	10.00
Plate, 9½″, dinner	12.00	20.00
Plate, 10″, grill	8.00	14.00
Plate, 10″, service	8.50	16.00
Plate, 12½″, service	9.00	17.50
Relish, 6 inserts	65.00	95.00
Salt dip, 1½″, ftd.	10.00	17.50
Sauce boat & plate	45.00	65.00
Saucer	1.00	2.50
Stem, 1 oz., cordial	20.00	45.00
Stem, 3½ oz., cocktail	12.00	20.00
Stem, 6 oz., low sherbet	9.00	15.00
Stem, 6 oz., high sherbet	10.00	20.00
Stem, 9 oz., water	15.00	30.00
Sugar, lightning bolt handles	7.00	12.00
Sugar, ftd.	9.00	20.00
Sugar, scalloped edge	9.00	20.00
Sugar, tall, lg. ft.	8.00	18.00
Tray, 8″, 2 hdld., flat pickle	10.00	17.00
Tray, 9″, pickle	10.00	17.50
Tray, 11″, oval service	8.00	15.00
Tray, 11″, celery	10.00	20.00
Tray, 12″, oval service	10.00	20.00
Tray, 13″, 2 hdld. service	20.00	30.00
Tray, 15″, oval service	15.00	25.00
Tumbler, 2½ oz., ftd.	7.00	12.00
Tumbler, 5 oz., ftd.	8.00	15.00
Tumbler, 8 oz., ftd.	10.00	20.00
Tumbler, 10 oz., ftd.	12.00	22.00
Tumbler, 12 oz., ftd.	15.00	30.00

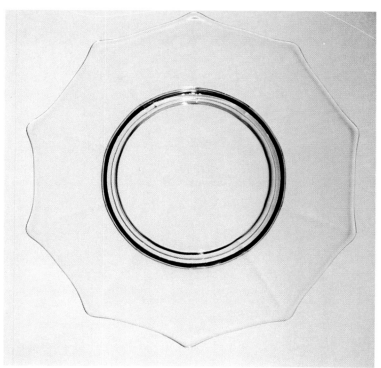

DIANE, Cambridge Glass Company, 1934 - Early 1950's

Colors: crystal, some pink, yellow, blue

This is another of the Cambridge patterns that has few collectors; but there are some really neat pieces that can be found in Diane. Has anyone got the green candy bottom I need? I guess I won't be redundant from the last book and mention the way my wife remembers Diane . . . Oh, well! You talked me into it. It reminds her of a cartoon mouse, complete with "ears" and a big nose!

Add 20% to 25% for colors.

	Crystal
Basket, 6", 2 hdld, ftd.	16.00
Bowl, #3106, finger w/liner	25.00
Bowl, #3122, finger w/liner	25.00
Bowl, #3400, cream soup w/liner	22.00
Bowl, 5", berry	20.00
Bowl, 5¼", 2 hdld. bonbon	18.00
Bowl, 6", 2 hdld. ftd. bonbon	17.00
Bowl, 6", 2 pt. relish	18.00
Bowl, 6", cereal	22.50
Bowl, 6½", 3 pt. relish	20.00
Bowl, 7", 2 hdld. ftd. bonbon	22.00
Bowl, 7", 2 pt. relish	20.00
Bowl, 7", relish or pickle	20.00
Bowl, 9", 3 pt. celery & relish	30.00
Bowl, 9½", pickle (like corn)	22.00
Bowl, 10", 4 ft. flared	35.00
Bowl, 10", baker	35.00
Bowl, 11", 2 hdld.	35.00
Bowl, 11", 4 ftd.	40.00
Bowl, 11½", tab hdld., ftd.	40.00
Bowl, 12", 3 pt. celery & relish	32.50
Bowl, 12", 4 ft.	40.00
Bowl, 12", 4 ft. flared	40.00
Bowl, 12", 4 ft. oval	42.00
Bowl, 12", 4 ft. oval w/"ears" hdl.	47.00
Bowl, 12", 5 pt. celery & relish	32.50
Butter, rnd.	95.00
Cabinet flask	125.00
Candelabrum, 2-lite, keyhole	22.50
Candelabrum, 3-lite, keyhole	27.50
Candlestick, 1-lite, keyhole	17.50
Candlestick, 5"	17.50
Candlestick, 6", 2-lite "fleur-de-lis"	27.50
Candlestick, 6", 3-lite	32.50
Candy box w/cover, rnd.	65.00
Cigarette urn	32.00
Cocktail shaker, glass top	95.00
Cocktail shaker, metal top	65.00
Cocktail icer, 2 pc.	32.50
Comport, 5½"	22.00
Comport, 5⅜", blown	35.00
Creamer	14.00
Creamer, indiv. #3500 (pie crust edge)	14.00
Creamer, indiv. #3900, scalloped edge	14.00
Creamer, scroll handle #3400	14.00
Cup	15.00
Decanter, lg. ftd.	125.00
Decanter, short ft. cordial	150.00
Hurricane lamp, candlestick base	90.00
Hurricane lamp, keyhole base w/prisms	125.00
Ice bucket w/chrome hand.	60.00
Mayonnaise, div., w/liner & ladles	30.00
Mayonnaise (sherbet type w/ladle)	27.50
Mayonnaise w/liner, ladle	25.00
Oil, 6 oz., w/stopper	39.00
Pitcher, ball	95.00
Pitcher, Doulton	195.00
Pitcher, upright	125.00

57

DIANE, Cambridge Glass Company, 1934 - Early 1950's (continued)

	Crystal
Plate, 6″, 2 hdld. plate	7.00
Plate, 6″, sq. bread/butter	5.00
Plate, 6½″, bread/butter	5.00
Plate, 8″, 2 hdld. ftd. bonbon	11.00
Plate, 8″, salad	8.00
Plate, 8½″	8.00
Plate, 10½″, dinner	45.00
Plate, 12″, 4 ft. service	35.00
Plate, 13″, 4 ft. torte	35.00
Plate, 13½″, 2 hdld.	28.00
Plate, 14″, torte	38.00
Platter, 13½″	45.00
Salt & pepper, ftd. w/glass tops, pr.	32.00
Salt & pepper, pr., flat	28.00
Saucer	5.00
Stem, #1066, 1 oz. cordial	42.50
Stem, #1066, 3 oz. cocktail	16.00
Stem, #1066, 3 oz. wine	20.00
Stem, #1066, 3½ oz. tall cocktail	17.50
Stem, #1066, 4½ oz. claret	17.50
Stem, #1066, 5 oz. oyster/cocktail	12.00
Stem, #1066, 7 oz. low sherbet	11.50
Stem, #1066, 7 oz. tall sherbet	13.50
Stem, #1066, 11 oz. water	15.00
Stem, #3122, 1 oz. cordial	45.00
Stem, #3122, 2½ oz., wine	20.00
Stem, #3122, 3 oz., cocktail	14.00
Stem, #3122, 4½ oz., claret	19.00
Stem, #3122, 4½ oz., oyster/cocktail	15.00
Stem, #3122, 7 oz., low sherbet	11.00
Stem, #3122, 7 oz., tall sherbet	15.00
Stem, #3122, 9 oz., water goblet	18.00
Sugar, indiv., #3500 (pie crust edge)	13.00
Sugar, indiv., #3900, scalloped edge	13.00
Sugar, scroll handle #3400	14.00
Tumbler, 2½ oz., sham bottom	25.00
Tumbler, 5 oz. ft. juice	27.00
Tumbler, 5 oz., sham bottom	27.00
Tumbler, 7 oz., old fashioned w/sham bottom	29.00
Tumbler, 8 oz. ft.	22.00
Tumbler, 10 oz. sham bottom	27.00
Tumbler, 12 oz. sham bottom	30.00
Tumbler, 13 oz.	30.00
Tumbler, 14 oz. sham bottom	35.00
Tumbler, #1066, 3 oz.	14.00
Tumbler, #1066, 5 oz., juice	11.00
Tumbler, #1066, 9 oz., water	12.00
Tumbler, #1066, 12 oz., tea	12.50
Tumbler, #3106, 3 oz., ftd.	13.00
Tumbler, #3106, 5 oz., ftd., juice	13.00
Tumbler, #3106, 9 oz., ftd. water	11.00
Tumbler, #3106, 12 oz., ftd. tea	12.00
Tumbler, #3122, 2½ oz.	14.00
Tumbler, #3122, 5 oz., juice	13.00
Tumbler, #3122, 9 oz., water	15.00
Tumbler, #3122, 12 oz., tea	17.00
Tumbler, #3135, 2½ oz., ft. bar	16.00
Tumbler, #3135, 10 oz. ft. tumbler	14.00
Tumbler, #3135, 12 oz. ft. tea	15.00
Vase, 5″, globe	25.00
Vase, 6″, high ft. flower	22.00
Vase, 8″, high ft. flower	22.00
Vase, 9″, keyhole base	35.00
Vase, 10″, bud	20.00
Vase, 11″, flower	32.50
Vase, 11″, ped. ft. flower	45.00
Vase, 12″, keyhole base	40.00
Vase, 13″, flower	50.00

Note: See Page 148-149 for stem identification.

ELAINE, Cambridge Glass Company, 1934 - 1950's

Colors: crystal

A late 1940's magazine advertisement describes this pattern as being "exquisite as bridal lace" and shows a bride beneath a frothy bridal veil admiring this crystal.

An entire listing of #3104 stems has not been priced because I have not seen any sell. The catalogs list them as having been made; so, I include the listing here for your information.

	Crystal		Crystal
Basket, 6", 2 hdld. (upturned sides)	15.00	Stem, #1402, 1 oz. cordial	42.50
Bowl, #3104, finger w/liner	20.00	Stem, #1402, 3 oz., wine	22.00
Bowl, 5¼", 2 hdld. bonbon	12.50	Stem, #1402, 3½ oz., cocktail	20.00
Bowl, 6", 2 hdld., ftd. bonbon	15.00	Stem, #1402, 5 oz., claret	20.00
Bowl, 6", 2 pt. relish	15.00	Stem, #1402, low sherbet	14.00
Bowl, 6½", 3 pt. relish	14.00	Stem, #1402, tall sherbet	15.00
Bowl, 7", 2 pt. pickle or relish	15.50	Stem, #1402, goblet	20.00
Bowl, 7", ftd. tab hdld. bonbon	25.00	Stem, #3104, (very tall stems),	
Bowl, 7", pickle or relish	17.50	¾ oz. brandy	----
Bowl, 9", 3 pt. celery & relish	20.00	Stem, #3104, 1 oz., cordial	----
Bowl, 9½", pickle (like corn dish)	20.00	Stem, #3104, 1 oz., pousse-cafe	----
Bowl, 10", 3 ftd, flared	29.50	Stem, #3104, 2 oz., sherry	----
Bowl, 11", tab hdld.	22.50	Stem, #3104, 2½ oz., creme de menthe	----
Bowl, 11½", ftd., tab hdld.	27.50	Stem, #3104, 3 oz., wine	----
Bowl, 12", 3 pt. celery & relish	27.50	Stem, #3104, 3½ oz., cocktail	----
Bowl, 12", 4 ftd. flared	27.50	Stem, #3104, 4½ oz., claret	----
Bowl, 12", 4 ftd. oval, "ear" hdld.	32.50	Stem, #3104, 5 oz., roemer	----
Bowl, 12", 5 pt. celery & relish	32.50	Stem, #3104, 5 oz., tall hock	----
Candlestick, 5"	17.50	Stem, #3104, 7 oz., tall sherbet	----
Candlestick, 6", 2-lite	25.00	Stem, #3104, 9 oz., goblet	----
Candlestick, 6", 3-lite	30.00	Stem, #3121, 1 oz., cordial	45.00
Candy box w/cover, rnd.	50.00	Stem, #3121, 3 oz., cocktail	22.00
Cocktail icer, 2 pc.	30.00	Stem, #3121, 3½ oz., wine	25.00
Comport, 5½"	30.00	Stem, #3121, 4½ oz., claret	20.00
Comport, 5⅜", #3500 stem	37.50	Stem, #3121, 4½ oz., oyster cocktail,	
Comport, 5⅜", blown	35.00	low stem	15.00
Creamer	11.00	Stem, #3121, 5 oz., parfait, low stem	25.00
Creamer, indiv.	10.00	Stem, #3121, 6 oz., low sherbet	15.00
Cup	16.00	Stem, #3121, 6 oz., tall sherbet	17.50
Decanter, lg., ftd.	120.00	Stem, #3121, 10 oz., water	21.00
Hurricane lamp, candlestick base	70.00	Stem, #3500, 1 oz., cordial	45.00
Hurricane lamp, keyhole ft. w/prisms	110.00	Stem, #3500, 2½ oz., wine	22.00
Ice bucket w/chrome handle	57.50	Stem, #3500, 3 oz., cocktail	20.00
Mayonnaise, (cupped "sherbet" w/ladle)	22.00	Stem, #3500, 4½ oz., claret	20.00
Mayonnaise (div. bowl, liner, 2 ladles)	30.00	Stem, #3500, 4½ oz., oyster cocktail	
Mayonnaise, w/liner & ladle	25.00	low stem	14.00
Oil, 6 oz., hdld. w/stopper	40.00	Stem, #3500, 5 oz., parfait, low stem	22.00
Pitcher, ball	80.00	Stem, #3500, 7 oz., low sherbet	13.00
Pitcher, Doulton	195.00	Stem, #3500, 7 oz., tall sherbet	15.00
Pitcher, upright	125.00	Stem, #3500, 10 oz., water	20.00
Plate, 6", 2 hdld.	10.00	Sugar	10.00
Plate, 6½", bread/butter	6.50	Sugar, indiv.	10.00
Plate, 8", 2 hdld., ftd.	15.00	Tumbler, #1402, 9 oz., ftd. water	16.00
Plate, 8", salad	12.50	Tumbler, #1402, 12 oz., tea	18.00
Plate, 8", tab hdld. bonbon	15.00	Tumbler, #1402, 12 oz., tall ftd. tea	20.00
Plate, 10½", dinner	40.00	Tumbler, #3121, 5 oz., ftd. juice	18.00
Plate, 11½", 2 hdld., ringed "Tally		Tumbler, #3121, 10 oz., ftd. water	20.00
Ho" sand.	25.00	Tumbler, #3121, 12 oz., ftd. tea	22.00
Plate, 12", 4 ftd. service	25.00	Tumbler, #3500, 5 oz., ftd. juice	16.00
Plate, 13", 4 ftd. torte	30.00	Tumbler, #3500, 10 oz., ftd. water	18.00
Plate, 13½", tab hdld. cake	30.00	Tumbler, #3500, 12 oz., ftd. tea	20.00
Plate, 14", torte	30.00	Vase, 6", ftd.	20.00
Salt & pepper, pr.	27.50	Vase, 8", ftd.	30.00
Saucer	3.00	Vase, 9", keyhole, ftd.	35.00

Note: See Pages 148-149 for stem identification.

EMPRESS, Blank #1401, A. H. Heisey & Co.

Colors: crystal, "Flamingo" pink, "Sahara" yellow, "Moongleam" green, cobalt and "Alexandrite"; some Tangerine

Most non-collectors of Empress are "impressed" by the dolphin feet on the footed items. The pitcher is marked, and if you can't find the mark, try looking on the inside of one of the dolphin feet!

	Crystal	Flam.	Sahara	Moon.	Cobalt	Alexan.
Ash Tray	25.00	40.00	50.00	60.00	125.00	130.00
Bonbon, 6″	10.00	15.00	17.00	20.00		
Bowl, cream soup	10.00	15.00	20.00	30.00		
Bowl, cream soup w/sq. liner	15.00	20.00	25.00	35.00		165.00
Bowl, frappe w/center	15.00	25.00	35.00	45.00		
Bowl, nut, dolphin ftd., indiv.	15.00	22.00	25.00	30.00		80.00
Bowl, 4½″, nappy	5.00	8.00	10.00	12.50		
Bowl, 5″, preserve, 2 hdld.	10.00	15.00	20.00	25.00		
Bowl, 6″, ftd., jelly, 2 hdld.	12.00	17.00	23.00	27.50		
Bowl, 6″, dolp. ftd. mint	12.00	17.00	22.00	27.50		90.00
Bowl, 6″, grapefruit, sq. top, grnd. bottom	7.00	10.00	15.00	20.00		
Bowl, 6½″, oval lemon w/cover	35.00	55.00	65.00	75.00		
Bowl, 7″, 3 pt. relish, triplex	12.00	18.00	22.00	25.00		
Bowl, 7″, 3 pt. relish, ctr. hand.	15.00	25.00	27.50	30.00		
Bowl, 7½″ dolp. ftd. nappy	25.00	55.00	60.00	65.00	260.00	310.00
Bowl, 7½″, dolp. ftd. nasturtium	25.00	60.00	65.00	70.00	310.00	375.00
Bowl, 8″, nappy	22.00	30.00	35.00	40.00		
Bowl, 8½″, ftd., floral, 2 hdld.	25.00	40.00	50.00	60.00		
Bowl, 9″, floral, rolled edge	22.00	30.00	35.00	40.00		
Bowl, 9″, floral, flared	30.00	60.00	65.00	70.00		
Bowl, 10″, 2 hdld. oval dessert	27.00	35.00	45.00	55.00		
Bowl, 10″, lion head, floral	225.00	500.00	450.00	550.00		
Bowl, 10″, oval veg.	27.00	35.00	45.00	55.00		
Bowl, 10″, square salad, 2 hdld.	27.00	35.00	45.00	55.00		
Bowl, 10″, triplex relish	15.00	25.00	30.00	35.00		
Bowl, 11″, dolphin ftd. floral	25.00	60.00	65.00	70.00	310.00	375.00
Bowl, 13″, pickle/olive, 2 pt.	10.00	15.00	18.00	25.00		
Bowl, 15″, dolp. ftd. punch	225.00	500.00	550.00	600.00		
Candlestick, low, 4 ftd. w/2 hand.	15.00	35.00	40.00	45.00		
Candlestick, 6″, dolphin ftd.	30.00	55.00	60.00	75.00	175.00	
Candy w/cover, 6″, dolphin ftd.	35.00	85.00	90.00	95.00		
Comport, 6″, ftd.	25.00	40.00	55.00	65.00		
Comport, 6″, square	35.00	65.00	70.00	75.00		
Comport, 7″, oval	33.00	60.00	66.00	70.00		
Compotier, 6″, dolphin ftd.	60.00	125.00	165.00	185.00		
Creamer, dolphin ftd.	15.00	25.00	35.00	38.00		200.00
Creamer, indiv.	15.00	25.00	35.00	40.00		200.00
Cup	8.00	26.00	30.00	35.00		97.50
Cup, after dinner	12.50	30.00	35.00	45.00		
Cup, bouillon, 2 hdld.	15.00	25.00	28.00	30.00		
Cup, 4 oz. custard or punch	10.00	25.00	28.00	30.00		
Cup #1401½, has rim as demi-cup	12.00	26.00	30.00	35.00		
Grapefruit w/square liner	12.00	20.00	25.00	30.00		
Ice tub w/metal handles	35.00	85.00	95.00	110.00		
Jug, 3 pint, ftd.	60.00	160.00	170.00	185.00		
Marmalade w/cover, dolp. ftd.	30.00	45.00	60.00	70.00		
Mayonnaise, 5½″, ftd.	20.00	35.00	45.00	50.00		150.00
Mustard w/cover	30.00	60.00	65.00	75.00		
Oil bottle, 4 oz.	30.00	65.00	90.00	100.00		

63

	Crystal	Flam.	Sahara	Moon.	Cobalt	Alexan.
Plate, bouillon liner	4.00	7.00	10.00	12.00		
Plate, cream soup liner	5.00	9.00	13.00	15.00		
Plate, 4½″	2.00	5.00	6.00	7.00		
Plate, 6″	5.00	10.00	13.00	15.00		35.00
Plate, 6″, square	5.00	10.00	13.00	15.00		35.00
Plate, 7″	7.00	12.00	15.00	17.00		45.00
Plate, 7″, square	7.00	12.00	15.00	17.00		45.00
Plate, 8″, square	9.00	16.00	20.00	24.00	60.00	60.00
Plate, 8″	9.00	16.00	20.00	24.00	60.00	60.00
Plate, 9″	12.00	25.00	35.00	40.00		
Plate, 10½″	20.00	45.00	55.00	60.00		
Plate, 10½″, square	20.00	45.00	55.00	60.00		125.00
Plate, 12″	25.00	45.00	55.00	60.00		
Plate, 12″, muffin, sides upturned	30.00	50.00	60.00	65.00		
Plate, 13″, hors d'oeuvre, 2hdld.	26.00	32.50	40.00	47.50		
Plate, 13″, square, 2 hdld.	26.00	32.50	40.00	47.50		
Platter, 14″	22.00	32.50	37.50	42.50		
Salt & pepper, pr.	40.00	70.00	90.00	100.00		225.00
Saucer, square	3.00	8.00	14.00	16.00		22.50
Saucer, after dinner	2.00	7.00	10.00	10.00		
Saucer	3.00	8.00	14.00	16.00		
Stem, 2½ oz., oyster cocktail	15.00	20.00	25.00	30.00		
Stem, 4 oz., saucer champagne	20.00	25.00	30.00	35.00		
Stem, 4 oz., sherbet	15.00	20.00	25.00	30.00		
Stem, 9 oz., Empress stemware, unusual	25.00	32.00	42.00	52.00		
Sugar, indiv.	15.00	25.00	35.00	40.00		200.00
Sugar, dolphin ftd. 3 hdld.	10.00	22.00	25.00	27.00		200.00
Tray, condiment & line for indiv. sugar/creamer	10.00	15.00	20.00	23.00		
Tray, 10″, 3 pt. relish	18.00	25.00	30.00	35.00		
Tray, 10″, 7 pt. hors d'oeuvre	25.00	30.00	35.00	40.00		
Tray, 10″, celery	12.00	16.00	22.00	26.00		150.00
Tray, 12″, ctr. hdld sand.	30.00	48.00	57.00	65.00		
Tray, 12″, sq. ctr. hdld. sand.	30.00	48.00	57.00	65.00		
Tray, 13″, celery	14.00	18.00	24.00	28.00		
Tray, 16″, 4 pt. buffet relish	20.00	25.00	30.00	35.00		
Tumbler, 8 oz., dolp. ftd., unusual	60.00	85.00	120.00	125.00		
Tumbler, 8 oz., grnd. bottom	12.00	17.00	24.00	27.00		
Tumbler, 12 oz., tea, grnd. bottom	15.00	20.00	27.00	30.00		
Vase, 8″, flared	45.00	65.00	75.00	85.00		
Vase, 9″, ftd.	50.00	90.00	100.00	135.00		525.00

FAIRFAX, Fostoria Glass Company, 1927 - 1944

Colors: blue, orchid, amber, rose, green, topaz, some ruby and black

Fairfax is actually the blank on which other Fostoria patterns (Versailles, June, Trojan) were etched. Naturally, being plain, there is not quite the demand for Fairfax as for the other patterns. On the other hand, people who prefer their dishes to form a background for food, enjoy the simplicity of Fairfax. Blue, in particular, seems to have caught the eye of the modern day collector.

As with the other patterns, pitchers, footed oils, salt and pepper shakers and the salad dresing bottles are choice pieces to own.

Due to extreme confusion by some collectors and some dealers alike, I have shown on page 69 all of the Fostoria stems so that differences in shapes can be seen. Never again should anyone confuse the high sherbet with the claret just because they are the same height. Note the claret is shaped like the wine.

	Blue, Orchid	Amber, Rose	Green, Topaz		Blue, Orchid	Amber, Rose	Green, Topaz
Ash tray	20.00	13.00	17.50	Plate, canape	5.00	3.00	4.00
Baker, 9″, oval	22.50	15.00	20.00	Plate, 6″, bread/butter	3.00	2.00	2.50
Baker, 10½″, oval	30.00	20.00	22.50	Plate, 7″, salad	5.00	3.00	3.50
Bonbon	11.00	8.00	9.00	Plate, 7″, cream soup liner	5.00	3.00	3.50
Bottle, salad dressing	----	60.00	70.00	Plate, 8″, salad	6.00	4.50	5.00
Bouillon, ftd.	11.00	7.00	8.00	Plate, 9½″, luncheon	8.00	5.00	6.00
Bowl, lemon, 2 hdld.	7.00	5.00	6.00	Plate, 10¼″, dinner	17.50	12.00	13.50
Bowl, whipped cream	11.00	8.00	9.00	Plate, 10¼″, grill	12.00	8.00	10.00
Bowl, 5″, fruit	8.00	5.00	6.00	Plate, 10″, cake	17.50	13.00	15.00
Bowl, 6″, cereal	13.50	8.00	10.00	Plate, 12″, bread	14.00	10.00	12.00
Bowl, 7″, soup	15.00	10.00	12.00	Plate, 14″, torte	17.50	14.00	15.00
Bowl, 8″, rnd. nappy	17.50	12.00	13.50	Platter, 10½″, oval	22.00	15.00	17.50
Bowl, lg., hdld. dessert	15.00	10.00	12.00	Platter, 15″, oval	35.00	25.00	30.00
Bowl, 12″	20.00	15.00	18.00	Relish, 8½″	10.00	7.00	8.00
Bowl, 12″, centerpiece	22.00	17.50	20.00	Relish, 11½″	15.00	10.00	12.00
Bowl, 13″, oval centerpiece	25.00	20.00	22.50	Sauce boat	30.00	20.00	25.00
Bowl, 15″, centerpeice	27.50	20.00	24.00	Sauce boat liner	12.00	9.00	10.00
Butter dish w/cover	125.00	80.00	90.00	Saucer, after dinner	6.00	4.00	5.00
Candlestick, flattened top	12.00	10.00	10.00	Saucer	4.00	2.50	3.00
Candlestick, 3″	11.50	9.00	10.00	Shaker, ftd., pr.	50.00	30.00	35.00
Celery, 11½″	16.00	12.00	14.00	Shaker, indiv., ft., pr.	----	20.00	25.00
Cheese & cracker, set	25.00	20.00	22.50	Stem, 4″, ¾ oz., cordial	40.00	25.00	30.00
Comport, 7″	15.00	10.00	12.00	Stem, 4¼″, 6 oz., low sherbet	12.00	11.00	11.00
Cream soup, ftd.	12.00	9.00	8.00	Stem, 5¼″, 3 oz., cocktail	20.00	15.00	18.00
Creamer, flat	----	10.00	12.00	Stem, 5½″, 3 oz., wine	25.00	22.50	22.50
Creamer, ftd.	11.00	7.00	9.00	Stem, 6″, 4 oz., claret	20.00	18.00	18.00
Creamer, tea	13.00	7.00	9.00	Stem, 6″, 6 oz., high sherbet	13.00	12.50	12.50
Cup, after dinner	15.00	10.00	12.50	Stem, 8¼″, 10 oz., water	20.00	17.50	18.00
Cup, flat	----	4.00	6.00	Sugar, flat	----	10.00	12.00
Cup, ftd.	8.00	6.00	7.00	Sugar, ftd.	10.00	6.00	8.00
Flower holder, oval	25.00	18.00	20.00	Sugar cover	30.00	20.00	22.50
Ice bucket	40.00	30.00	35.00	Sugar, tea	12.50	6.00	8.00
Mayonnaise	12.00	9.00	10.00	Sweetmeat	11.00	7.00	9.00
Mayonnaise ladle	12.00	6.00	6.00	Tray, 11″, ctr. hand.	20.00	12.00	15.00
Mayonnaise liner, 7″	5.00	3.00	3.50	Tumbler, 4½″, 5 oz., ftd.	12.00	10.00	11.00
Oil, ftd.	100.00	75.00	85.00	Tumbler, 5¼″, 9 oz., ftd.	13.50	12.00	12.50
Pickle, 8½″	10.00	7.00	9.00	Tumbler, 6″, 12 oz., ftd.	15.00	13.50	14.00
Pitcher	150.00	110.00	120.00				

See page 69 for stem identification.

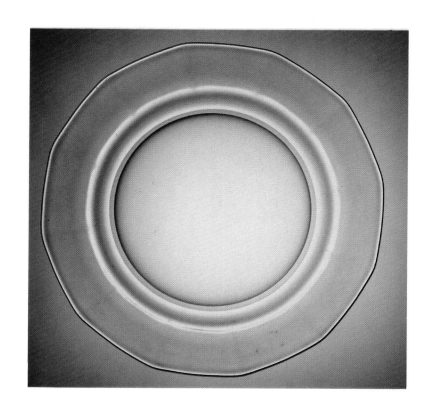

FOSTORIA STEMS AND SHAPES

Top Row: Left to Right:
1. Water, 10 oz., 8¼″
2. Claret, 4 oz., 6″
3. Wine, 3 oz., 5½″
4. Cocktail, 3 oz., 5¼″
5. Sherbet, high, 6″
6. Sherbet, low, 4¼″
7. Cordial, ¾ oz., 4″

Bottom Row:Left to Right:
1. Ice tea, 12 oz., 6″
2. Water, 9 oz., 5¼″
3. Parfait, 5¼″
4. Juice, 5 oz., 4½″
5. Bar, 2½ oza. ·
6. Oyster cocktail, 5½ oz.
7. Grapefruit and liner

FLANDERS, Tiffin Glass Company, 1920's - mid 1930's

Colors: crystal, pink, yellow

Flanders has become one of Tiffin's most collected Depression Era patterns. Note that its stems as with its sister pattern, Cadena, are crystal with colored bowls. You may find additional items not listed. Prices for the crystal will be 25% to 30% less than the prices listed.

Believe it or not, the cup and saucer are very hard to find.

	Pink/ Yellow		Pink/ Yellow
Bowl, finger w/liner	20.00	Plate, 9½", dinner	35.00
Bowl, 2 hdld., bonbon	17.50	Relish, 3 pt.	27.50
Bowl, 12", flanged rim console	27.50	Saucer	7.50
Candlestick	20.00	Stem, cordial	47.50
Celery, 11"	25.00	Stem, cocktail	22.50
Comport, 3½"	17.50	Stem, oyster cocktail	15.00
Comport, 6"	27.50	Stem, parfait	30.00
Creamer, ftd.	17.50	Stem, saucer, champagne	15.00
Cup	22.50	Stem, sherbet	12.50
Grapefruit w/liner	32.50	Stem, water	22.50
Mayonnaise, w/liner	37.50	Stem, wine	32.50
Oil bottle & stopper	97.50	Sugar, ftd.	16.50
Pitcher & cover	250.00	Tumbler, 9 oz., ftd. water	15.00
Plate, 6"	7.50	Tumbler, 12 oz., ftd. tea	22.50
Plate, 7½"	10.00		

FUCHSIA Tiffin Glass Company, Late 1930's - early 1940's

Colors: crystal

As with Flanders, the cup and saucer are very hard to find; but this is one of the few patterns that the cordial seems to have been made abundantly. In fact, stemware is more readily available in both of these patterns than any of the serving pieces.

	Crystal		Crystal
Bowl, finger w/liner	15.00	Plate, 9½", dinner	22.50
Bowl, 2 hdld., bonbon	12.50	Relish, 3 pt.	20.00
Bowl, 12", flanged rim console	22.50	Saucer	4.50
Candlestick	15.00	Stem, cordial	32.50
Celery, 11"	17.50	Stem, cocktail	15.00
Comport, 6"	19.50	Stem, oyster cocktail	12.50
Creamer, ftd.	15.00	Stem, parfait	20.00
Cup	20.00	Stem, saucer champagne	12.50
Mayonnaise, w/liner	27.50	Stem, sherbet	10.00
Pitcher & cover	150.00	Stem, water	22.50
Plate, 6"	5.00	Stem, wine	27.50
Plate, 7½"	7.50	Sugar, ftd.	14.00
Plate, 8½"	12.50	Tumbler, 9 oz., ftd. water	12.50

GLORIA, (etching 1746), Cambridge Glass 3400 Line Dinnerware Introduced 1930

Colors: crystal, yellow, pink, green, emerald green, amber, Heatherbloom

There seems to be more yellow Gloria available than any other color. For some reason I am attracted to the emerald green in this pattern and I normally do not give green a second look. The creamer and cup in the foreground are Cambridge's Heatherbloom color which is similar to Heisey's Alexandrite.

The Heatherbloom and emerald green will fetch prices of 20% to 25% higher than the prices listed for other colors.

	Crystal	Colors		Crystal	Colors
Basket, 6″, 2 hdld. (sides up)	12.00	18.00	Comport, 4″, fruit cocktail	10.00	16.50
Bowl, 3″, indiv. nut, 4 ftd.	20.00	30.00	Comport, 5″, 4 ftd.	15.00	30.00
Bowl, 3½″, cranberry, 4 ftd.	12.50	30.00	Comport, 6″, 4 ftd.	17.00	32.50
Bowl, 5″, ftd., crimped edge bonbon	14.00	20.00	Comport, 7″, low	25.00	40.00
Bowl, 5″, sq. fruit "saucer"	7.00	13.00	Comport, 7″, tall	32.00	60.00
Bowl, 5½″, bonbon, 2 hdld.	14.00	20.00	Comport, 9½″, tall, 2 hdld., ftd bowl	55.00	97.50
Bowl, 5½″, bonbon ftd.,	12.00	17.50	Creamer, ftd.	11.00	16.00
Bowl, 5½″, flattened, ftd. bonbon	12.00	17.50	Creamer, tall, ftd.	11.00	17.50
Bowl, 5½″, fruit "saucer"	7.50	12.50	Cup, rnd., or sq.	12.00	20.00
Bowl, 6″, rnd. cereal	9.00	15.00	Cup, 4 ftd. sq.	17.00	30.00
Bowl, 6″, sq. cereal	9.00	14.50	Cup, after dinner (demitasse), rnd. or sq.	25.00	35.00
Bowl, 8″, 2 pt., 2 hdld. relish	15.00	22.50	Fruit cocktail, 6 oz., ftd. (3 styles)	9.00	15.00
Bowl, 8″, 3 pt., 3 hdld. relish	20.00	32.50	Ice pail, metal handle w/tongs	37.50	65.00
Bowl, 8¾″, 2 hdld., figure "8" pickle	17.50	25.00	Mayonnaise w/liner & ladle, (4 ftd. bowl)	30.00	50.00
Bowl, 8¾″, 2 pt., 2 hdld. figure "8" relish	20.00	30.00	Oil w/stopper; tall, ftd., hdld.	60.00	110.00
Bowl, 9″, salad, tab hdld.	20.00	37.50	Oyster cocktail, #3035, 4½ oz.	10.00	15.00
Bowl, 9½″, 2 hdld., veg.	50.00	75.00	Oyster cocktail, 4½ oz., low stem	10.00	15.00
Bowl, 10″, oblong, tab hdld. "baker"	22.50	30.00	Pitcher, 67 oz., middle indent	90.00	195.00
Bowl, 10″, 2 hdld.	30.00	55.00	Pitcher, 80 oz., ball	75.00	145.00
Bowl, 11″, 2 hdld. fruit	27.00	50.00	Pitcher w/cover, 64 oz.	70.00	140.00
Bowl, 12″, 4 ftd. console	22.50	40.00	Plate, 6″, 2 hdld.	8.00	13.50
Bowl, 12″, 4 ftd. flared rim	22.00	35.00	Plate, 6″, bread/butter	6.00	9.00
Bowl, 12″, 4 ftd. oval	30.00	55.00	Plate, 7½″, tea	7.00	11.00
Bowl, 12″, 5 pt. celery & relish	22.50	40.00	Plate, 8½″	8.00	13.00
Bowl, 13″, flared rim	22.50	35.00	Plate, 9½″ dinner	30.00	45.00
Bowl, cream soup w/rnd. liner	15.00	30.00	Plate, 10″, tab hdld. salad	15.00	30.00
Bowl, cream soup w/sq. saucer	15.00	30.00	Plate, 11″, 2 hdld.	15.00	22.50
Bowl, finger, flared edge w/rnd. plate	14.00	25.00	Plate, 11″, sq., ftd. cake	45.00	95.00
Bowl, finger, ftd.	12.00	22.50	Plate, 11½″, tab hdld. sandwich	17.50	30.00
Bowl, finger w/rnd. plate	15.00	30.00	Plate, 14″, chop or salad	35.00	50.00
Butter w/cover, 2 hdld.	80.00	165.00	Plate, sq. bread/butter	6.00	9.00
Candlestick, 6″, ea.	17.50	30.00	Plate, sq. dinner	30.00	45.00
Candy box w/cover, 4 ftd. w/tab hdld.	40.00	67.50	Plate, sq. salad	7.00	11.00
Cheese compote w/11½″ cracker plate, tab hdld.	25.00	42.50	Plate, sq. service	22.00	40.00
			Platter, 11½″	30.00	50.00
Cocktail shaker, grnd. stopper, spout (like pitcher)	70.00	150.00	Salt & pepper, pr., short	25.00	40.00
			Salt & pepper, pr., w/glass top, tall	27.50	60.00

73

GLORIA, (etching 1746), Cambridge Glass 3400 Line Dinnerware Introduced 1930, (continued)

	Crystal	Colors
Salt & pepper, ftd., metal tops	32.50	62.50
Saucer, rnd.	2.00	3.00
Saucer, rnd. after dinner	4.00	5.00
Saucer, sq., after dinner (demitasse)	4.00	5.00
Saucer, sq.	2.00	3.00
Stem, #3035, 2½ oz., wine	17.50	25.00
Stem, #3035, 3 oz., cocktail	17.50	25.00
Stem, #3035, 3½ oz., cocktail	17.00	24.00
Stem, #3035, 4½ oz., claret	17.50	24.00
Stem, #3035, 6 oz., low sherbet	10.00	15.00
Stem, #3035, 6 oz., tall sherbet	11.00	17.50
Stem, #3035, 9 oz., water	15.00	25.00
Stem, #3035, 3½ oz., cocktail	17.00	24.00
Stem, #3115, 9 oz., goblet	13.00	22.00
Stem, #3120, 1 oz., cordial	40.00	65.00
Stem, #3120, 4½ oz., claret	16.00	25.00
Stem, #3120, 6 oz., low sherbet	10.00	15.00
Stem, #3120, 6 oz., tall sherbet	11.00	16.00
Stem, #3120, 9 oz., water	15.00	22.50
Stem, #3130, 2½ oz., wine	16.00	25.00
Stem, #3130, 6 oz., low sherbet	10.00	15.00
Stem, #3130, 6 oz., tall sherbet	11.00	16.00
Stem, #3130, 8 oz., water	15.00	22.50
Stem, #3135, 1 oz., cordial	35.00	60.00
Stem, #3135, 6 oz., low sherbet	11.00	15.00
Stem, #3135, 6 oz., tall sherbet	12.00	16.00
Stem, #3135, 8 oz., water	15.00	22.50
Sugar, ftd.	11.00	16.00
Sugar, tall, ftd.	11.00	17.50
Sugar shaker w/glass top	65.00	145.00
Syrup, tall, ftd.	40.00	65.00
Tray, 11", ctr. hdld. sandwich	20.00	30.00

	Crystal	Colors
Tray, 2 pt. ctr. hdld. relish	22.00	35.00
Tray, 4 pt. ctr. hdld. relish	30.00	45.00
Tray, 9", pickle, tab hdld.	15.00	25.00
Tumbler, #3035, 5 oz., high ftd.	10.00	17.50
Tumbler, #3035, 10 oz., high ftd.	12.00	20.00
Tumbler, #3035, 12 oz., high ftd.	14.00	20.00
Tumbler, #3115, 5 oz., ftd. juice	12.00	17.50
Tumbler, #3115, 8 oz., ftd.	12.00	17.50
Tumbler, #3115, 10 oz., ftd.	13.00	18.50
Tumbler, #3115, 12 oz., ftd.	14.00	20.00
Tumbler, #3120, 2½ oz., ftd. (used w/cocktail shaker)	12.00	17.50
Tumbler, #3120, 5 oz., ftd.	12.00	17.50
Tumbler, #3120, 10 oz., ftd.	12.00	17.50
Tumbler, #3120, 12 oz., ftd.	14.00	20.00
Tumbler, #3120, 2½ oz., ftd. (used w/shaker)	12.00	17.50
Tumbler, #3130, 5 oz., ftd.	12.00	17.50
Tumbler, #3130, 10 oz., ftd.	12.00	17.50
Tumbler, #3130, 12 oz., ftd.	14.00	20.00
Tumbler, #3135, 5 oz., juice	12.00	17.50
Tumbler, #3135, 10 oz., water	12.00	17.50
Tumbler, #3135, 12 oz., tea	14.00	20.00
Tumbler, 12 oz., flat, (2 styles)-one w/indent side to match, 67 oz. pitcher	14.00	20.00
Vase, 9", oval, 4 indent	40.00	75.00
Vase, 10", keyhole base	35.00	60.00
Vase, 10", squarish top	32.00	55.00
Vase, 11"	35.00	60.00
Vase, 11", neck indent	35.00	60.00
Vase, 12", keyhole base, flared rim	40.00	75.00
Vase, 12", squarish top	37.50	67.50
Vase, 14", keyhole base, flared rim	45.00	82.50

Note: See Pages 148-149 for stem identification.

GREEK KEY, A. H. Heisey & Co.

Colors: Crystal, "Flamingo" pink punch bowl and cups only

	Crystal		Crystal
Bowl, finger	15.00	Pitcher, 1 pint	55.00
Bowl, Jelly w/cover, 2 hdld. ftd.	125.00	Pitcher, 1 quart	60.00
Bowl, indiv. ftd. almond	25.00	Pitcher, 3 pint	75.00
Bowl, 4″, nappy	10.00	Pitcher, ½ gal.	85.00
Bowl, 4″, shallow, low ft., jelly	15.00	Oil bottle, 2 oz., squat w/#8 stopper	57.50
Bowl, 4½″, nappy	15.00	Oil bottle, 2 oz., w/#6 stopper	62.50
Bowl, 4½″, scalloped nappy	17.50	Oil bottle, 4 oz., squat w/#8 stopper	67.50
Bowl, 4½″, shallow, low ft., jelly	14.00	Oil bottle, 4 oz., w/#6 stopper	72.50
Bowl, 5″, ftd. almond	32.50	Oil bottle, 6 oz., w/#6 stopper	82.50
Bowl, 5″, ftd. almond w/cover	85.00	Oil bottle, 6 oz., squat w/#8 stopper	77.50
Bowl, 5″, hdld. jelly	35.00	Plate, 4½″	10.00
Bowl, 5″, low ft. jelly w/cover	40.00	Plate, 5″	11.00
Bowl, 5″, nappy	22.50	Plate, 5½″	11.00
Bowl, 5½″, nappy	25.00	Plate, 6″	12.00
Bowl, 5½″, shallow nappy, ftd.	55.00	Plate, 6½″	12.00
Bowl, 6″, nappy	25.00	Plate, 7″	13.00
Bowl, 6″, shallow nappy	27.50	Plate, 8″	15.00
Bowl, 6½″, nappy	28.00	Plate, 9″	20.00
Bowl, 7″, low ft., straight side	32.50	Plate, 10″	45.00
Bowl, 7″, nappy	30.00	Plate, 16″, orange bowl liner	50.00
Bowl, 8″, low ft., straight side	37.50	Puff box, #1 w/cover	60.00
Bowl, 8″, nappy	35.00	Puff box, #3 w/cover	70.00
Bowl, 8″, scalloped nappy	40.00	Salt & pepper, pr.	60.00
Bowl, 8″, shallow, low ft.	42.50	Sherbet, 4½ oz., ftd., straight rim	12.50
Bowl, 8½″, shallow nappy	42.50	Sherbet, 4½ oz., ftd., flared rim	12.50
Bowl, 9″, flat banana split	19.00	Sherbet, 4½ oz., hi. ft., shallow	12.50
Bowl, 9″, ftd. banana split	20.00	Sherbet, 4½ oz., ftd., shallow	12.50
Bowl, 9″, low ft., straight side	42.50	Sherbet, 4½ oz., ftd., cupped rim	12.50
Bowl, 9″, nappy	40.00	Sherbet, 6 oz., low ft.	13.00
Bowl, 9″, shallow, low ft.	45.00	Spooner, lg.	65.00
Bowl, 9½″, shallow nappy	42.50	Spooner, 4½″, (or straw jar)	75.00
Bowl, 10″, shallow, low ft.	45.00	Stem, ¾ oz., cordial	165.00
Bowl, 11″, shallow nappy	48.00	Stem, 2 oz., wine	130.00
Bowl, 12″, orange bowl	50.00	Stem, 2 oz., sherry	120.00
Bowl, 12″, punch, ftd.	165.00	Stem, 3 oz., cocktail	20.00
(Flamingo)	650.00	Stem, 3½ oz., burgundy	90.00
Bowl, 14″, orange, flared rim	62.50	Stem, 4½ oz., saucer champagne	20.00
Bowl, 14½″, orange, flared rim	60.00	Stem, 4½ oz., claret	87.50
Bowl, 15″, punch, ftd.	120.00	Stem, 7 oz.	60.00
Bowl, 18″, punch, shallow	130.00	Stem, 9 oz.	70.00
Butter, indiv. (plate)	15.00	Stem, 9 oz., low ft.	60.00
Butter/jelly, 2 hdld. w/cover	170.00	Straw jar w/cover	250.00
Candy w/cover, ½ lb.	110.00	Sugar	25.00
Candy w/cover, 1 lb.	120.00	Sugar, oval, hotel	30.00
Candy w/cover, 2 lb.	150.00	Sugar, rnd., hotel	27.50
Cheese & cracker set, 10″	55.00	Sugar & creamer, oval, individual	65.00
Compote, 5″	50.00	Tray, 9″, oval celery	17.50
Compote, 5″, w/cover	60.00	Tray, 12″, oval celery	20.00
Creamer	25.00	Tray, 12½″, French roll	55.00
Creamer, oval, hotel	30.00	Tray, 13″, oblong	60.00
Creamer, rnd., hotel	27.50	Tray, 15″, oblong	62.50
Cup, 4½ oz., punch	18.00	Tumbler, 2½ oz., (or toothpick)	250.00
(Flamingo)	30.00	Tumbler, 5 oz., flared rim	17.50
Egg cup, 5 oz.	50.00	Tumbler, 5 oz., straight side	17.50
Hair receiver	55.00	Tumbler, 5½ oz., water	18.00
Ice tub, lg., tab hdld.	65.00	Tumbler, 7 oz., flared rim	20.00
Ice tub, sm., tab hdld.	50.00	Tumbler, 7 oz., straight side	22.00
Ice tub w/cover, hotel	75.00	Tumbler, 8 oz., w/straight, flared, cupped, shallow	25.00
Ice tub w/cover, 5″, individual w/5″ plate	75.00	Tumbler, 10 oz., flared rim	27.00
Jar, 1 qt., crushed fruit w/cover	175.00	Tumbler, 10 oz., staight wide	27.00
Jar, 2 qt., crushed cruit w/cover	225.00	Tumbler, 12 oz., flared rim	28.00
Jar, lg. cover horseradish	67.50	Tumbler, 12 oz., straight side	28.00
Jar, sm. cover horseradish	57.50	Tumbler, 13 oz., straight side	29.00
Jar, tall celery	62.00	Tumbler, 13 oz., flared rim	30.00
Jar w/knob cover, pickle	82.50	Water bottle	95.00

IMPERIAL HUNT SCENE, #718, Cambridge Glass Company, Late 1920's - 1930's

Colors: amber, black, crystal, Emerald green; green, pink

This pattern caught my wife's eye several years ago, but it has taken more than a little searching to find much of it. Collectors have always enjoyed patterns with animals on them and this one has horses and dogs running along its edges. Since we are only about 10 miles from the Kentucky Horse Park, it doesn't take much to see a lot of collecting possibilities for Hunt Scene in this area. However, there is so little available here in Kentucky that we have to do most of our searching in the Ohio area where it was made.

Much of this pattern is found on Cambridge's 1402 line which is more than apropos since this line is also known as Tally-Ho.

Prices for black and emerald green will be about 25% higher than the prices listed below. You will probably find more pieces than what are listed here. Let me know what you find!

	All Colors
Bowl, 6″, cereal	17.50
Bowl, 8″	35.00
Bowl, 8½″, 3 pt.	37.50
Candlestick, 2-lite, keyhole	25.00
Candlestick, 3-lite, keyhole	35.00
Creamer, ftd.	25.00
Ice bucket	55.00
Ice tub	50.00
Mayonnaise, w/liner	45.00
Pitcher, w/cover, 63 oz., #3077	175.00
Pitcher, w/cover, 76 oz., #711	150.00
Plate, 8″	20.00
Stem, 1 oz., cordial #1402	50.00
Stem, 2½ oz., wine #1402	35.00
Stem, 3 oz., cocktail #1402	25.00
Stem, 6 oz., tomato #1402	20.00
Stem, 6½ oz., sherbet #1402	15.00
Stem, 7½ oz., sherbet #1402	20.00
Stem, 10 oz., water #1402	25.00
Stem, 14 oz., #1402	30.00
Stem, 18 oz., #1402	40.00
Stem, 1 oz., cordial #3077	50.00
Stem, 2½ oz., cocktail #3077	25.00
Stem, 6 oz., low sherbet #3077	17.50
Stem, 6 oz., high sherbet #3077	20.00
Stem, 9 oz., water #3077	25.00
Sugar, ftd.	22.50
Tumbler, 2½ oz., flat, #1402	15.00
Tumbler, 5 oz., flat, #1402	15.00
Tumbler, 7 oz., flat, #1402	20.00
Tumbler, 10 oz., flat, #1402	22.50
Tumbler, 10 oz., flat, tall, #1402	25.00
Tumbler, 15 oz., flat, #1402	32.50
Tumbler, 2½ oz., ftd., #3077	15.00
Tumbler, 5 oz., ftd., #3077	17.50
Tumbler, 8 oz., ftd., #3077	20.00
Tumbler, 10 oz., ftd., #3077	22.50
Tumbler, 12 oz., ftd., #3077	25.00

79

IPSWICH, Blank #1405, A. H. Heisey & Co.

Colors: crystal, "Flamingo" pink, "Sahara" yellow, "Moongleam" green, cobalt and "Alexandrite"

Look on page 152 or 153 if you think you have a piece of Alexandrite. I received more letters from readers saying that they had candy dishes in Ipswich in the Alexandrite color than any one item in the first book. What you are finding is Imperial's Heather made from the Heisey mold from 1961-1965. These were also made in amber, antique blue, and verde (green). To confuse matters even more, the tumbler was made with a plain Cambridge lid in Moonlight blue and Mandarin gold (yellow).

Only Heisey made crystal, pink, yellow and the green. The Imperial verde green is very yellow green compared to Heisey Moongleam. If you wish to be better informed about what Heisey pieces were made by Imperial, I suggest you write the Heisey Club (see page 158) for their book *Heisey By Imperial*.

	Crystal	Pink	Sahara	Green	Cobalt	Alexan.
Bowl, finger w/underplate	20.00	45.00	40.00	45.00		
Bowl, 11", ft. floral	35.00				275.00	
Candlestick, 6", 1-lite	75.00	200.00	150.00	190.00	310.00	
Candlestick centerpiece, ft., vase, "A"						
prisms	95.00	240.00	225.00	300.00	450.00	
Candy jar, ½ lb., w/cover	45.00	165.00	225.00	275.00		
Cocktail shaker, 1 quart, strainer #86						
stopper	160.00	260.00	260.00	475.00		
Creamer.	17.00	30.00	32.50	37.50		
Stem, 4 oz., oyster cocktail.	8.00					
Stem, 5 oz., saucer champagne	12.50					
Stem, 10 oz., goblet	18.00					650.00
Stem, 12 oz., schoppen	27.50					
Pitcher, ½ gal.	125.00	200.00	300.00	500.00	650.00	
Oil bottle, 2 oz., ft. #86 stopper	65.00	165.00	125.00	165.00		
Plate, 7", square.	15.00	20.00	22.00	25.00		
Plate, 8", square.	16.00	22.00	24.00	27.00		
Sherbet, 4 oz.	7.00	17.50	22.50	27.50		
Sugar	17.00	40.00	35.00	40.00		
Tumbler, 5 oz., ft.	9.00	30.00	25.00	30.00		
Tumbler, 8 oz., ft.	10.00	32.00	27.50	32.50		
Tumbler, 10 oz., cupped rim	12.50	35.00	30.00	35.00		
Tumbler, 10 oz., straight rim	12.50	35.00	30.00	35.00		
Tumbler, 12 oz., ft.	14.00	45.00	40.00	45.00		

JUNE, Fostoria Glass Company, 1928 - 1944

Colors: crystal; "Azure" blue, "Topaz" yellow, "Rose" pink

This is one of the most highly collected of the Fostoria patterns. Choice pieces to own include the pitcher, footed oils, shakers with those glass lids, cordials, 2½ oz., tumblers and the grapefruits with liners. Blue, again, seems the color most eagerly sought by collectors today.

	Crystal	Blue	Rose, Topaz		Crystal	Blue	Rose, Topaz
Ash tray	22.00	35.00	30.00	Grapefruit liner	20.00	50.00	40.00
Bottle, salad dressing,				Ice bucket	47.50	90.00	75.00
sterling top	135.00	275.00	245.00	Ice dish	21.00	42.50	37.50
Bowl, baker, 9″, oval	31.50	55.00	45.00	Ice dish liner (tomato,			
Bowl, bonbon	12.50	20.00	17.50	crab, fruit)	5.00	10.00	7.50
Bowl, bouillon, ftd.	12.00	25.00	20.00	Mayonnaise w/liner	22.50	45.00	37.50
Bowl, finger w/liner	32.50	35.00	45.00	Oil, ftd.	150.00	325.00	235.00
Bowl, lemon	14.00	25.00	18.00	Oyster cocktail, 5½ oz.	16.00	30.00	23.00
Bowl, mint	10.00	20.00	15.00	Parfait, 5¼″	20.00	45.00	35.00
Bowl, 5″, fruit	11.00	21.00	17.50	Pitcher	195.00	400.00	300.00
Bowl, 6″, cereal	15.00	27.50	22.50	Plate, canape	10.00	18.00	15.00
Bowl, 6″, nappy, ftd.	10.00	23.00	18.00	Plate, 6″, bread/butter	4.50	6.00	5.00
Bowl, 7″, nappy	15.00	23.00	20.00	Plate, 6″, finger bowl			
Bowl, 7″, soup	17.50	35.00	25.00	liner	4.50	6.00	5.00
Bowl, lg., dessert, hdld.	20.00	45.00	27.50	Plate, 7″, salad	5.00	10.00	8.00
Bowl, 10″	20.00	47.50	35.00	Plate, 7½″, cream soup	4.00	9.00	7.50
Bowl, 10″, Grecian	30.00	55.00	50.00	Plate, 8¾″, luncheon	6.00	12.00	10.00
Bowl, 11″, centerpiece	20.00	50.00	35.00	Plate, 9½″, sm. dinner	8.00	18.00	15.00
Bowl, 12″, centerpiece,				Plate, 10″, grill	16.00	32.00	27.50
several types	25.00	60.00	42.50	Plate, 10″, cake, hdld.	20.00	45.00	35.00
Bowl, 13″, oval				Plate, 10¼″, dinner	20.00	42.00	35.00
centerpiece	30.00	66.00	45.00	Plate, 13″, chop	20.00	42.00	35.00
Candlestick, 2″	10.00	20.00	15.00	Platter, 12″	20.00	42.00	35.00
Candlestick, 3″	12.00	21.50	17.50	Platter, 15″	25.00	75.00	55.00
Candlestick, 3″, Grecian	15.00	22.50	20.00	Relish, 8½″	14.00	22.00	20.00
Candlestick, 5″	12.50	22.00	20.00	Sauce boat	32.50	80.00	60.00
Candy w/cover, 3 pt.	45.00	125.00	85.00	Sauce boat liner	7.50	20.00	12.50
Candy w/cover, ½ lb.	50.00	135.00	90.00	Saucer, after dinner	6.00	10.00	8.00
Celery, 11½″	25.00	40.00	35.00	Saucer	4.00	7.50	5.00
Cheese & cracker, set	25.00	57.50	40.00	Shaker, ftd. pr.	60.00	130.00	92.50
Comport, 5″	18.00	32.50	27.50	Sherbet, high, 6″, 6 oz.	17.50	29.00	25.00
Comport, 6″	20.00	40.00	26.00	Sherbet, low, 4¼″, 6 oz.	15.00	25.00	20.00
Comport, 7″	22.00	45.00	27.50	Sugar, ftd.	12.00	25.00	22.00
Comport, 8″	24.00	40.00	35.00	Sugar cover	45.00	150.00	100.00
Cream soup, ftd.	12.00	35.00	30.00	Sugar pail	60.00	135.00	110.00
Creamer, ftd.	12.00	20.00	16.00	Sugar, tea	15.00	35.00	30.00
Creamer, tea	15.00	35.00	30.00	Tray, 11″, ctr. hdld.	20.00	45.00	35.00
Cup, after dinner	20.00	45.00	35.00	Tumbler, 2½ oz., ftd.	20.00	40.00	35.00
Cup, ftd.	15.00	27.50	22.00	Tumbler, 5 oz., 4½″, ftd.	15.00	27.50	22.50
Decanter	125.00	300.00	250.00	Tumbler, 9 oz., 5¼″, ftd.	15.00	27.50	21.50
Goblet, claret, 6″, 4 oz.	30.00	55.00	50.00	Tumbler, 12 oz., 6″, ftd.	17.50	30.00	25.00
Goblet, cocktail, 5¼″, 3 oz.	20.00	32.50	30.00	Vase, 8″	60.00	145.00	125.00
Goblet, cordial, 4″, ¾ oz.	40.00	77.50	65.00	Vase, 8½″, fan ftd.	50.00	110.00	90.00
Goblet, water, 8¼″ 10 oz.	21.00	33.00	28.00	Whipped cream bowl	10.00	15.00	12.50
Goblet, wine, 5½″, 3 oz.	22.00	52.50	45.00	Whipped cream pail	55.00	115.00	100.00
Grapefruit	25.00	60.00	50.00				

Note: See page 69 for stem identification.

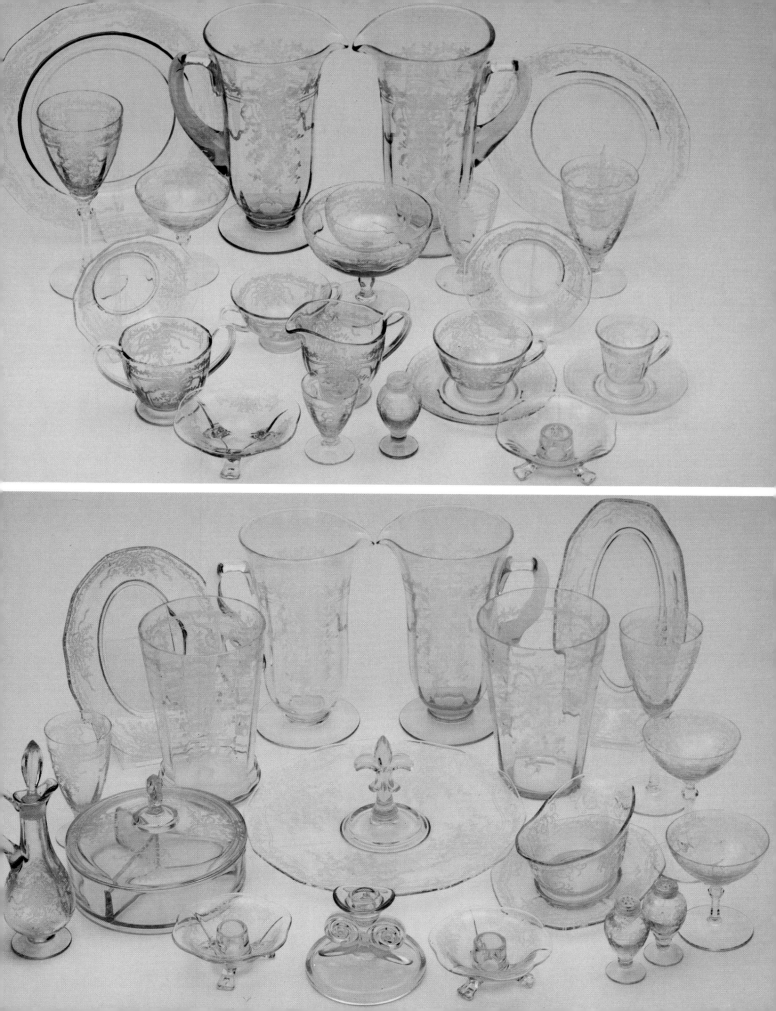

KASHMIR, Fostoria Glass Company, 1930 - 1934

Colors: "Topaz" yellow, green; some blue

There are few collectors for blue Kashmir and even less blue is available than there are collectors for it. Add 50% to the prices listed below for the blue. I will leave the blank spaces again and hope that some of these listed stems will turn up this time.

	Yellow, Green		Yellow, Green
Ash tray	25.00	Plate, 9", luncheon	9.00
Bowl, cream soup	20.00	Plate, 10", dinner	30.00
Bowl, finger	15.00	Plate, 10", grill	22.00
Bowl, 5", fruit	12.00	Plate, cake, 10"	-----
Bowl, 6", cereal	20.00	Salt and pepper	85.00
Bowl, 7", soup	25.00	Sandwich, center hdld.	35.00
Bowl, 8½", pickle	16.00	Sauce boat w/liner	75.00
Bowl, 9", baker	35.00	Saucer, rnd.	5.00
Bowl, 10"	40.00	Saucer, sq.	5.00
Bowl, 12", centerpiece	40.00	Saucer, after dinner, rnd.	6.00
Candlestick, 2"	15.00	Stem, ¾ oz., cordial	75.00
Candlestick, 3"	20.00	Stem, 2½ oz., ftd.	25.00
Candlestick, 5"	22.50	Stem, 2 oz., ftd. whiskey	25.00
Candlestick, 9½"	40.00	Stem, 2½ oz., wine	30.00
Candy w/cover	65.00	Stem, 3 oz., cocktail	22.00
Cheese and cracker set	50.00	Stem, 3½ oz., ftd. cocktail	22.00
Comport, 6"	32.50	Stem, 4 oz., claret	28.00
Creamer, ftd.	17.50	Stem, 4½ oz., oyster cocktail	16.00
Cup	15.00	Stem, 5½ oz., parfait	-----
Cup, after dinner, flat	22.50	Stem, 5 oz., ftd. juice	15.00
Cup, after dinner, ftd.	22.50	Stem, 5 oz., low sherbet	13.00
Grapefruit	35.00	Stem, 6 oz., high sherbet	17.50
Grapefruit liner	25.00	Stem, 9 oz., water	-----
Ice bucket	65.00	Stem, 10 oz., ftd. water	-----
Oil, ftd.	225.00	Stem, 11 oz.	-----
Pitcher, ftd.	350.00	Stem, 12 oz., ftd.	-----
Plate, 6", bread and butter	5.00	Stem, 13 oz., ftd. tea	-----
Plate, 7", salad, rnd.	6.00	Stem, 16 oz., ftd. tea	-----
Plate, 7", salad, sq.	6.00	Sugar, ftd.	15.00
Plate, 8", salad	8.00	Vase, 8"	75.00

Note: See stemware identification on page 69.

LARIAT, Blank #1540, A. H. Heisey & Co.

Colors: crystal; rare in black

	Crystal		Crystal
Ash tray, 4″	7.50	Oil bottle, 4 oz., hdld. w/#133 stopper	65.00
Basket, 7½″, bonbon	80.00	Oil bottle, 6 oz., oval	47.50
Basket, 8½″, ftd.	125.00	Plate, 6″, finger bowl liner	5.00
Basket, 10″, ftd.	150.00	Plate, 7″, salad	7.00
Bowl, 7 quart punch	85.00	Plate, 8″, salad	9.00
Bowl, 4″, nut	14.00	Plate, 11″, cookie	20.00
Bowl, 7″, 2 pt. relish	16.00	Plate, 12″, demi-torte, rolled edge	22.50
Bowl, 7″, nappy	13.00	Plate, 13″, deviled egg	120.00
Bowl, 8″, flat nougat	13.00	Plate, 14″, 2 hdld. sandwich	32.50
Bowl, 9½″, camellia	17.50	Plate, 21″, buffet	50.00
Bowl, 10″, hdld. celery	26.00	Platter, 15″, oval	27.50
Bowl, 10½″, 2 hdld. salad	27.50	Salt & pepper, pr.	160.00
Bowl, 10½″, salad	27.50	Saucer	5.00
Bowl, 11″, 2 hdld., oblong relish	18.00	Stem, 1 oz., cordial, double loop	150.00
Bowl, 12″, floral or fruit	16.00	Stem, 1 oz., cordial blown	135.00
Bowl, 13″, celery	18.00	Stem, 2½ oz., wine, blown	20.00
Bowl, 13″, gardenia	20.00	Stem, 3½ oz., cocktail, pressed	10.00
Bowl, 13″, oval floral	25.00	Stem, 3½ oz., cocktail, blown	10.00
Candlestick, 1-lite	10.00	Stem, 3½ oz., wine, pressed	10.00
Candlestick, 2-lite	15.00	Stem, 4 oz., claret, blown	15.00
Candlestick, 3-lite	25.00	Stem, 4¼ oz., oyster cocktail or fruit	10.00
Candy box w/cover	35.00	Stem, 4½ oz., oyster cocktail, blown	10.00
Candy w/cover, 7″	40.00	Stem, 5½ oz., sherbet/saucer champagne blown	12.00
Cheese, 5″, ftd. w/cover	27.50	Stem, 6 oz., low sherbet	7.00
Cheese dish w/cover 8″	40.00	Stem, 6 oz., sherbet/saucer champagne, pressed	9.00
Cigarette box	22.50	Stem, 9 oz., pressed	15.00
Coaster, 4″	7.50	Stem, 10 oz., blown	15.00
Compote, 10″, w/cover	60.00	Sugar	12.00
Creamer	12.50	Tray for sugar & creamer	15.00
Creamer & sugar w/tray, indiv.	35.00	Tumbler, 5 oz., ftd. juice	10.00
Cup	12.00	Tumbler, 5 oz., ftd., juice, blown	10.00
Cup, punch	5.00	Tumbler, 12 oz., ftd. iced tea	15.00
Ice tub	60.00	Tumbler, 12 oz., ftd. iced tea, blown	15.00
Jar w/cover, 12″, urn	125.00	Vase, 7″, ftd. fan	27.50
Lamp & globe, 7″, black-out	75.00		
Lamp & globe, 8″, candle	65.00		
Mayonnaise, 5″ bowl, 7″ plate	32.50		

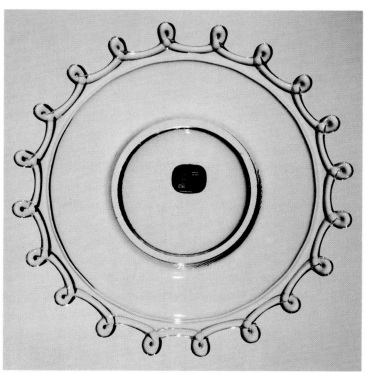

MINUET, Etch 1530, QUEEN ANN Blank, #1509; TOUJOURS Blank, #1511; SYMPHONE Blank, #5010,

et. al.; 1939 - 1950's

Colors: crystal

I've found a few more pieces of Minuet since the first book. In fact I have been looking at eight parfaits in one shop for over two years. They are still there because the dealer fails to see that they are not cordials as he has them listed and priced.

	Crystal		Crystal
Bell, dinner	40.00	Plate, 7″, salad	12.00
Bowl, finger, #3309	15.00	Plate, 7″, salad #1511 TOUJOURS	14.00
Bowl, 6″, ftd. mint	12.00	Plate, 8″, luncheon	17.50
Bowl, 6″, ftd., 2 hdld. jelly	17.50	Plate, 8″, luncheon #1511 TOUJOURS	19.00
Bowl, 6½″, salad dressings	22.50	Plate, 10½″, service	45.00
Bowl, 7″, salad dressings	25.00	Plate, 12″, rnd., 2 hdld. sandwich	45.00
Bowl, 7″, triplex relish	22.50	Plate, 13″, floral salver #1511 TOUJOURS	40.00
Bowl, 7½″, sauce, ftd.	24.00	Plate, 14″, torte, #1511 TOUJOURS	37.50
Bowl, 9½″, 3 pt., "5 o'clock" relish	32.50	Plate, 15″, sand., #1511 TOUJOURS	40.00
Bowl, 10″, salad, #1511, TOUJOURS	35.00	Plate, 16″, Snack rack w/1477 2-lite candle	60.00
Bowl, 11″, 3 pt., "5 o'clock" relish	40.00	Salt & pepper, pr. (#10)	45.00
Bowl, 11″, ftd. floral	42.50	Saucer	5.00
Bowl, 12″, oval floral, #1511 TOUJOURS	42.50	Stem, #5010, SYMPHONE, 1 oz., cordial	135.00
Bowl, 12″, oval, #1514	42.50	Stem, #5010, 2½ oz., wine	60.00
Bowl, 13″, floral, #1511 TOUJOURS	40.00	Stem, #5010, 3½ oz., cocktail	40.00
Bowl, 13″, pickle & olive	25.00	Stem, #5010, 4 oz., claret	40.00
Bowl, 13½″, shallow salad	30.00	Stem, #5010, 4½ oz., oyster cockail	30.00
Candelabrum, 1-lite w/prisms	110.00	Stem, #5010, 6 oz., saucer champagne	30.00
Candelabrum, 2-lite, bobeche & prisms	100.00	Stem, #5010, 6 oz., sherbet	17.50
Candlestick, 1-lite, #112	20.00	Stem, #5010, 9 oz., water	30.00
Candlestick, 3-lite, #142 CASCADE	55.00	Sugar, indiv. #1511 TOUJOURS	25.00
Candlestick, 5″, 2-lite, #134 TRIDENT	45.00	Sugar, indiv. #1509 QUEEN ANN	22.50
Centerpiece vase & prisms #1511		Sugar, dolp. ft. #1509 QUEEN ANN	40.00
TOUJOURS	165.00	Sugar, #1511 TOUJOURS	35.00
Cocktail icer w/liner #3304 UNIVERSAL	35.00	Tray, 12″, celery #1511 TOUJOURS	30.00
Comport, 5½″, #5010	32.50	Tray, 15″, social hour	42.50
Comport, 7½″, #1511 TOUJOURS	70.00	Tray for indiv. sugar & creamer	15.00
Creamer, #1511	35.00	Tumbler, #5010, 5 oz., fruit juice	22.50
Creamer, dolp. ft.	40.00	Tumbler, #5010, 9 oz., low ftd. water	28.00
Creamer, indiv. #1509	25.00	Tumbler, #5010, 12 oz., tea	32.50
Creamer, indiv. #1511	30.00	Tumbler, #2351, 12 oz., tea	32.50
Cup	25.00	Vase, 5″, #5013	20.00
Ice bucket, dolp. ft.	110.00	Vase, 5½″, ftd. #1511 TOUJOURS	40.00
Marmalade w/cover, #1511 TOUJOURS		Vase, 6″, urn #5012	30.00
(apple shape)	65.00	Vase, 7½″, urn #5012	40.00
Mayonnaise, 5½″, dolp. ft.	30.00	Vase, 8″, #4196	40.00
Mayonnaise, ftd. #1511 TOUJOURS	35.00	Vase, 9″, urn #5012	50.00
Pitcher, 73 oz., #4164	150.00	Vase, 10″, #4192	60.00
Plate, 7″, mayonnaise liner	12.00	Vase, 10″, #4192, SATURN optic	75.00

89

MT. VERNON, Cambridge Glass Company, late 1920's - 1940's

Colors: amber, crystal, red, blue, Heatherbloom

This large Cambridge line is beginning to be collected. My prices are for amber and crystal with the other colors bringing up to 50% more.

	Amber/ Crystal		Amber/ Crystal
Ash tray, 3½″, #63	7.00	Decanter, 40 oz., w/stopper, #52	55.00
Ashtray, 4″, #68	10.00	Honey jar w/cover (marmalade), #74	25.00
Ash tray, 6″ x 4½″, oval, #71	10.00	Ice bucket, w/tongs, #92	30.00
Bon bon, 7″, ftd., #10	12.50	Lamp, 9″ hurricane, #1607	50.00
Bottle, bitters, 2½ oz., #62	50.00	Mayonnaise, divided, 2 spoons, #107	25.00
Bottle, 7 oz., sq. toilet, #18	60.00	Mug, 14 oz., stein, #84	22.00
Bowl, finger, #23	10.00	Mustard, w/cover, 2½ oz., #28	22.00
Bowl, 4½″, fruit, #31	6.00	Pickle, 6″, 1 hdld., #78	12.00
Bowl, 4½″, ivy ball or rose, ftd., #12	25.00	Pitcher, 50 oz., #90	50.00
Bowl, 5¼″, fruit, #6	10.00	Pitcher, 66 oz., #13	60.00
Bowl, 6″, cereal, #32	12.00	Pitcher, 80 oz., ball, #95	70.00
Bowl, 6″, preserve, #76	12.00	Pitcher, 86 oz., #91	75.00
Bowl, 6½″, rose, #106	18.00	Plate, finger bowl liner, #23	4.00
Bowl, 8″, pickle, #65	15.00	Plate, 6″, bread & butter, #4	3.00
Bowl, 8½″, 4 pt., 2 hdld. sweetmeat, #105	25.00	Plate, 6⅜″, bread & butter, #19	4.00
Bowl, 10″, 2 hdld., #39	20.00	Plate, 8½″, salad, #5	7.00
Bowl, 10½″, deep, #43	25.00	Plate, 10½″, dinner, #40	20.00
Bowl, 10½″, salad, #120	25.00	Plate, 11½″, tab hdld., #37	20.00
Bowl, 11″, oval, 4 ftd., #136	27.50	Relish, 6″, 2 pt., 2 hdld., 6″106	12.00
Bowl, 11″, oval, #135	25.00	Relish, 8″, 2 pt., hdld., #101	17.50
Bowl, 11½″, belled, #128	25.00	Relish, 8″, 3 pt., 3 hdld., #103	20.00
Bowl, 11½″, belled, #68	25.00	Relish, 11″, 3 part, #200	22.50
Bowl, 11½″, shallow, #126	25.00	Relish, 12″, 2 part, #80	25.00
Bowl, 11½″, shallow cupped, #61	25.00	Relish, 12″, 5 part, #104	25.00
Bowl, 12″, flanged, rolled edge, #129	30.00	Salt, indiv., #24	6.00
Bowl, 12″, oblong, crimped, #118	30.00	Salt, oval, 2 hdld., #102	12.00
Bowl, 12″, rolled edge, crimped, #117	30.00	Salt & pepper, pr., #28	22.50
Bowl, 12½″, flanged, rolled edge, #45	30.00	Salt & pepper, pr., short, #88	20.00
Bowl, 12½″, flared, #121	32.00	Salt & pepper, tall, #89	25.00
Bowl, 12½″, flared, #44	32.00	Salt dip, #24	8.00
Bowl, 13″, shallow, crimped, #116	35.00	Sauce boat & ladle, tab hdld., #30-445	50.00
Box, 3″, w/cover, round, #16	20.00	Saucer, #7	7.50
Box, 4″, w/cover, sq., #17	25.00	Stem, 3 oz., wine, #27	12.50
Box, 4½″, w/cover, ftd., round, #15	30.00	Stem, 3½ oz., cocktail, #26	9.00
Butter tub, w/cover, #73	60.00	Stem, 4 oz., oyster cocktail, #41	9.00
Cake stand, 10½″, ftd., #150	30.00	Stem, 4½ oz., claret, #25	12.50
Candelabrum, 13½″, #38	40.00	Stem, 4½ oz., low sherbet, #42	7.50
Candlestick, 4″, #130	10.00	Stem, 6½ oz., tall sherbet, #2	9.00
Candlestick, 5″, 2-lite, #110	15.00	Stem, 10 oz., water, #1	12.50
Candlestick, 8″, #35	20.00	Sugar, ftd., #8	10.00
Candy, w/cover, 1 lb., ftd., #9	35.00	Sugar, indiv., #4	10.00
Celery, 10½″, #79	15.00	Sugar, #86	10.00
Celery, 11″, #98	17.50	Tray, for indiv., sugar and creamer, #4	10.00
Celery, 12″, #79	20.00	Tumbler, 1 oz., ftd. cordial, #87	22.00
Cigarette box, 6″, w/cover, oval, #69	25.00	Tumbler, 2 oz., whiskey, #55	10.00
Cigarette holder, #66	15.00	Tumbler, 3 oz., ftd. juice, #22	9.00
Coaster, 3″, plain, #60	5.00	Tumbler, 5 oz., #56	12.00
Coaster, 3″, ribbed, #70	5.00	Tumbler, 5 oz., ftd., #21	12.00
Cocktail icer, 2 pc., #85	22.50	Tumbler, 7 oz., old fashion, #57	14.00
Cologne, 2½ oz., w/stopper, #1340	25.00	Tumbler, 10 oz., ftd. water, #3	15.00
Comport, 4½″, #33	12.00	Tumbler, 10 oz., table, #51	12.00
Comport, 5½″, 2 hdld., #77	15.00	Tumbler, 10 oz., tall, #58	12.00
Comport, 6″, #34	15.00	Tumbler, 12 oz., barrel shape, #13	15.00
Comport, 6½″, #97	17.50	Tumbler, 12 oz., ftd. tea, #20	16.00
Comport, 6½″, belled, #96	20.00	Tumbler, 14 oz., barrel shape, #14	20.00
Comport, 7½″, #11	25.00	Tumbler, 14 oz., tall, #59	20.00
Comport, 8″, #81	25.00	Urn w/cover (same as candy), #9	35.00
Comport, 9″, oval, 2 hdld., #100	27.50	Vase, 5″, #42	15.00
Comport, 9½″, #99	27.50	Vase, 6″, crimped, #119	20.00
Creamer, ftd., #8	10.00	Vase, 6″, ftd., #50	25.00
Creamer, indiv., #4	10.00	Vase, 6½″, squat, #107	27.50
Creamer, #86	10.00	Vase, 7″, #58	30.00
Cup, #7	6.50	Vase, 7″, ftd., #54	35.00
Decanter, 11 oz., #47	35.00	Vase, 10″, ftd., #46	45.00

OCTAGON, Blank #1231 - Ribbed; also Blank 500 and Blank 1229, A. H. Heisey & Co.

Colors: crystal, "Flamingo" pink, "Sahara" yellow, "Moongleam" green; "Hawthorne" orchid; "Marigold", a deep, amber/yellow, and "Dawn"

	Crystal	Flam.	Sahara	Moon.	Hawth.	Marigold
Basket, 5″, #500	50.00	80.00	95.00	90.00	125.00	
Bonbon, 6″, sides up, #1229	5.00	8.00	10.00	12.00	15.00	
Bowl, cream soup, 2 hdld.	10.00	17.00	22.00	28.00	32.00	
Bowl, 5½″, jelly, #1229	5.00	8.00	10.00	12.00	15.00	
Bowl, 6″, mint, #1229	5.00	8.00	10.00	12.00	15.00	
Bowl, 6″, #500	12.00	17.00	19.00	20.00	25.00	
Bowl, 6½″, grapefruit	9.00	14.00	16.00	15.00	20.00	
Bowl, 8″, ftd., #1229	12.00	17.00	20.00	24.00	28.00	
Bowl, 9″, vegetable	10.00	18.00	20.00	25.00	40.00	
Bowl, 12½″, salad	12.00	18.00	22.00	27.00	40.00	
Candlestick, 3″, 1-lite	7.00	15.00	20.00	25.00	35.00	
Cheese dish, 6″, 2 hdld., #1229	5.00	8.00	10.00	12.00	15.00	
Creamer #500	5.00	12.00	16.00	17.00	22.00	
Creamer, hotel	7.00	12.00	15.00	18.00	25.00	
Cup, after dinner	6.00	12.00	17.00	22.00	27.50	
Dish, frozen dessert #500	7.00	10.00	14.00	12.00	22.00	35.00
Ice tub, #500	25.00	50.00	65.00	70.00	85.00	100.00
Mayonnaise, 5½″, ftd. #1229	10.00	14.00	16.00	18.00	22.00	
Plate, cream soup liner	3.00	5.00	7.00	9.00	12.00	
Plate, 6″	4.00	6.00	8.00	10.00	12.00	
Plate, 7″, bread	5.00	7.00	9.00	11.00	13.00	
Plate, 8″, luncheon	6.00	8.00	10.00	12.00	14.00	
Plate, 9″, soup	10.00	14.00	18.00	22.00	26.00	
Plate, 10″, sand., #1229	13.00	18.00	22.00	25.00	30.00	
Plate, 10″, muffin, #1229	15.00	20.00	24.00	27.00	32.00	
Plate, 10½″	15.00	20.00	27.00	29.00	32.00	
Plate, 10½″, ctr. hdld. sandwich	20.00	30.00	35.00	40.00	50.00	
Plate, 12″, muffin, #1229	17.00	23.00	28.00	30.00	35.00	
Plate, 13″, hors d'oeuvre #1229	15.00	20.00	25.00	30.00	35.00	
Plate, 14″	20.00	25.00	30.00	30.00	35.00	
Platter, 12¾″	20.00	30.00	35.00	40.00	50.00	
Saucer, after dinner	2.00	5.00	6.00	6.00	12.00	
Sugar #500	5.00	12.00	16.00	17.00	22.00	
Sugar, hotel	7.00	12.00	15.00	18.00	25.00	
Tray, 6″, oblong, #500	5.00	12.00	16.00	17.00	22.00	
Tray, 9″, celery	7.00	15.00	18.00	20.00	25.00	
Tray, 12″, celery	10.00	20.00	25.00	27.00	32.00	(Dawn)
Tray, 12″, 4 pt., #500	22.00	50.00	60.00	70.00	80.00	225.00

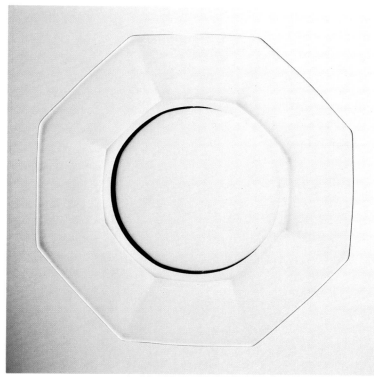

93

OLD COLONY, Empress Blank #1401; Caracassone Blank #3390; and Old Dominion Blank #3380, A. H. Heisey & Co., 1930 - 1939

Colors: Crystal, "Flamingo" pink, "Sahara" yellow, "Moongleam" green; "Marigold", a deep, amber/yellow; cobalt

	Crystal	Flam.	Sahara	Moon.	Marigold
Bouillion cup, 2 hdld., ftd.	12.00	17.00	19.00	22.00	
Bowl, finger, #4075	5.00	9.00	10.00	13.00	15.00
Bowl, ftd. finger, #3390	5.00	15.00	20.00	25.00	
Bowl, 4½", nappy	7.00	10.00	12.00	14.00	
Bowl, 5", ftd., 2 hdld.	12.00	17.00	22.00	27.00	
Bowl, 6", ftd., 2 hdld. jelly	14.00	19.00	24.00	30.00	
Bowl, 6", dolp. ftd. mint	15.00	20.00	25.00	32.50	
Bowl, 7", triplex relish	14.00	20.00	24.00	27.00	
Bowl, 7½", dolp. ftd. nappy	20.00	55.00	60.00	65.00	
Bowl, 8", nappy	24.00	33.00	38.00	40.00	
Bowl, 8½", ftd. floral, 2 hdld.	30.00	45.00	55.00	65.00	
Bowl, 9", 3 hdld.	35.00	70.00	80.00	85.00	
Bowl, 10", rnd., 2 hdld. salad	30.00	45.00	55.00	62.50	
Bowl, 10", sq. salad, 2 hdld.	30.00	45.00	55.00	62.50	
Bowl, 10", oval dessert, 2 hdld.	30.00	40.00	50.00	60.00	
Bowl, 10", oval veg.	30.00	34.00	42.00	50.00	
Bowl, 11", floral, dolp. ft.	30.00	65.00	70.00	75.00	
Bowl, 13", ftd. flared	28.00	34.00	38.00	42.00	
Bowl, 13", 2 pt. pickle & olive	12.00	18.00	20.00	25.00	
Cigarette holder #3390, (Cobalt $95.00)	15.00	45.00	40.00	50.00	
Comport, 7", oval, ftd.	35.00	65.00	70.00	75.00	
Comport, 7", ftd. #3368	30.00	55.00	60.00	80.00	75.00
Cream soup, 2 hdld.	12.00	18.00	20.00	25.00	
Creamer, dolp. ft.	17.50	30.00	42.50	47.50	
Creamer, indiv.	12.50	25.00	30.00	32.50	
Cup, after dinner	12.00	22.00	33.00	45.00	
Cup	10.00	26.00	32.00	38.00	
Decanter, 1 pt.	125.00	250.00	225.00	450.00	
Flagon, 12 oz., #3390	25.00	45.00	45.00	70.00	
Grapefruit, 6"	15.00	23.00	30.00	35.00	
Grapefruit, ftd. #3380	10.00	16.00	18.00	20.00	22.50
Ice tub, dolp. ft.	40.00	90.00	100.00	120.00	
Mayonnaise, 5½", dolp. ft.	36.00	55.00	70.00	80.00	
Oil, 4 oz., ftd.	40.00	65.00	100.00	110.00	
Pitcher, 3 pt., #3390	70.00	225.00	175.00	350.00	
Pitcher, 3 pt., dolp. ft.	65.00	150.00	165.00	175.00	
Plate, bouillon	5.00	8.00	12.00	15.00	
Plate, cream soup	5.00	8.00	12.00	15.00	
Plate, 4½", rnd.	3.00	6.00	7.00	8.00	
Plate, 6", rnd.	6.00	12.00	15.00	18.00	
Plate, 6", sq.	6.00	12.00	15.00	18.00	
Plate, 7", rnd.	8.00	14.00	18.00	20.00	
Plate, 7", sq.	8.00	14.00	18.00	20.00	
Plate, 8", rnd.	10.00	17.00	22.00	27.00	
Plate, 8", sq.	10.00	17.00	22.00	27.00	
Plate, 9", rnd.	15.00	22.00	25.00	28.00	
Plate, 10½", rnd.	25.00	50.00	60.00	67.50	
Plate, 10½", sq.	25.00	45.00	55.00	62.00	
Plate, 12", rnd.	30.00	55.00	65.00	70.00	
Plate, 12", 2 hdld. rnd. muffin	30.00	55.00	65.00	70.00	
Plate, 12", 2 hdld., rnd. sand.	30.00	55.00	65.00	70.00	
Plate, 13", 2 hdld., sq. sand.	35.00	40.00	45.00	50.00	
Plate, 13", 2 hdld., muffin, sq.	35.00	40.00	45.00	50.00	
Platter, 14", oval	25.00	35.00	40.00	45.00	
Salt & pepper, pr.	50.00	70.00	95.00	110.00	
Saucer, sq.	4.00	8.00	10.00	10.00	
Saucer, rnd.	4.00	8.00	10.00	10.00	
Stem, #3380, 1 oz., cordial	60.00	115.00	115.00	135.00	300.00
Stem, #3380, 2½ oz., wine	17.00	37.50	30.00	45.00	55.00
Stem, #3380, 3 oz., cocktail	13.00	34.00	25.00	40.00	50.00
Stem, #3380, 4 oz., oyster/cocktail	8.00	13.00	15.00	17.00	20.00
Stem, #3380, 4 oz., claret	17.00	40.00	30.00	45.00	55.00
Stem, #3380, 5 oz., parfait	10.00	15.00	15.00	17.00	35.00
Stem, #3380, 6 oz., champagne	8.00	13.00	15.00	17.00	20.00
Stem, #3380, 6 oz., sherbet	6.00	11.00	13.00	15.00	20.00
Stem, #3380, 10 oz., short soda	7.00	18.00	15.00	22.00	30.00

	Crystal	Flam.	Sahara	Moon.	Marigold
Stem, #3380, 10 oz., tall soda	-----	21.00	18.00	25.00	32.50
Stem, #3390, 1 oz., cordial	45.00	115.00	110.00	135.00	
Stem, #3390, 2½ oz., wine	12.00	20.00	27.50	35.00	
Stem, #3390, 3 oz., cocktail	7.00	15.00	20.00	25.00	
Stem, #3390, 3 oz., oyster/cocktail	7.00	15.00	20.00	25.00	
Stem, #3390, 4 oz., claret	12.00	22.50	27.50	32.50	
Stem, #3390, 6 oz., champagne	10.00	20.00	25.00	30.00	
Stem, #3390, 6 oz., sherbet	10.00	20.00	25.00	30.00	
Stem, #3390, 11 oz., low water	8.00	20.00	25.00	30.00	
Stem, #3390, 11 oz., tall water	10.00	22.00	27.00	32.00	
Sugar, dolp. ft.	17.50	30.00	42.40	47.50	
Sugar, indiv.	12.50	25.00	30.00	32.50	
Tray, 10″, celery..	14.00	20.00	25.00	30.00	
Tray, 12″, ctr. hdld. sand.	35.00	60.00	70.00	80.00	
Tray, 12″, ctr. hdld. sq.................................	35.00	60.00	70.00	80.00	
Tray, 13″, celery..	17.00	20.00	26.00	30.00	
Tray, 13″, 2 hdld. hors d'oeuvre	30.00	36.00	45.00	55.00	
Tumbler, dolp. ft.	75.00	100.00	135.00	150.00	
Tumbler, #3380, 1 oz., ftd. bar	22.00	35.00	40.00	50.00	50.00
Tumbler, #3380, 2 oz., ftd. bar	12.00	20.00	20.00	25.00	35.00
Tumbler, #3380, 5 oz., ftd. bar	7.00	12.00	12.00	17.00	25.00
Tumbler, #3380, 8 oz., ftd. soda.........................	10.00	21.00	18.00	25.00	32.50
Tumbler, #3380, 10 oz., ftd. soda........................	12.00	23.00	20.00	25.00	32.50
Tumbler, #3380, 12 oz., ftd. tea	13.00	25.00	22.00	27.00	35.00
Tumbler, #3390, 2 oz., ftd...............................	7.00	17.00	22.00	27.50	
Tumbler, #3390, 5 oz., ftd. juice	7.00	15.00	20.00	25.00	
Tumbler, #3390, 8 oz., ftd. soda	10.00	22.00	25.00	30.00	
Tumbler, #3390, 12 oz., ftd. tea	12.00	24.00	27.00	30.00	
Vase, 9″, ftd...	70.00	110.00	125.00	150.00	

OLD SANDWICH, Blank #1404, A. H. Heisey & Co.

Colors: Crystal, "Flamingo" pink, "Sahara" yellow, "Moongleam" green; cobalt

	Crystal	Flam.	Sahara	Moon.	Cobalt
Ash tray, individual	5.00	25.00	22.00	25.00	30.00
Beer mug, 12 oz.	25.00	190.00	200.00	250.00	275.00
Beer mug, 14 oz.	27.00	200.00	225.00	275.00	300.00
Beer mug, 18 oz.	29.00	225.00	250.00	300.00	350.00
Bottle, catsup w/#3 stopper (like lg. cruet)	30.00	60.00	75.00	80.00	
Bowl, finger	9.00	12.00	15.00	18.00	
Bowl, ftd. popped corn, cupped	30.00	45.00	55.00	65.00	
Bowl, 11", rnd. ftd., floral	25.00	40.00	50.00	60.00	
Bowl, 12", oval, ftd., floral	27.00	50.00	60.00	70.00	
Candlestick, 6"	28.00	50.00	60.00	70.00	200.00
Cigarette holder	27.50	35.00	40.00	45.00	
Comport, 6"	35.00	75.00	80.00	85.00	
Creamer, oval	7.00	20.00	22.00	25.00	
Creamer, 12 oz.	30.00	160.00	165.00	170.00	260.00
Creamer, 14 oz.	32.00	170.00	175.00	180.00	
Creamer, 18 oz.	35.00	180.00	185.00	190.00	
Cup	8.00	12.00	14.00	16.00	
Decanter, 1 pint w/#98 stopper	70.00	170.00	180.00	190.00	375.00
Floral block #22	15.00	25.00	30.00	35.00	
Oil bottle, 2½ oz., #85 stopper	60.00	80.00	85.00	90.00	
Parfait, 4½ oz.	10.00	15.00	20.00	25.00	
Pilsner, 8 oz.	14.00	28.00	32.00	38.00	
Pilsner, 10 oz.	16.00	30.00	35.00	40.00	
Pitcher, ½ gallon, ice	70.00	140.00	150.00	160.00	
Pitcher, ½ gallon, reg.	65.00	135.00	145.00	155.00	
Plate, 6", sq., grnd. bottom	4.00	8.00	10.00	13.00	
Plate, 7", sq.	5.00	10.00	13.00	15.00	
Plate, 8", sq.	7.00	12.00	15.00	17.00	
Salt & pepper, pr.	35.00	55.00	65.00	75.00	
Saucer	7.00	10.00	12.00	14.00	
Stem, 2½ oz., wine	12.00	22.00	30.00	35.00	
Stem, 3 oz., cocktail	9.00	15.00	18.00	20.00	
Stem, 4 oz., claret	10.00	18.00	20.00	25.00	125.00
Stem, 4 oz., oyster cocktail	5.00	10.00	12.00	15.00	
Stem, 4 oz., sherbet	6.00	12.00	15.00	18.00	
Stem, 5 oz., saucer champagne	8.00	25.00	27.00	30.00	
Stem, 10 oz., low ft.	9.00	25.00	30.00	35.00	
Sugar, oval	8.00	20.00	22.00	25.00	
Sundae, 6 oz.	5.00	10.00	15.00	20.00	
Tumbler, 1½ oz., bar, grnd. bottom	12.00	28.00	32.00	40.00	
Tumbler, 5 oz., juice	5.00	13.00	17.50	22.00	
Tumbler, 6½ oz., toddy	8.00	15.00	18.00	20.00	
Tumbler, 8 oz., grnd. bottom, cupped and straight rim	9.00	17.00	22.00	27.50	
Tumbler, 10 oz.	10.00	17.00	22.00	27.50	
Tumbler, 10 oz., low ft.	10.00	17.00	22.00	27.50	
Tumbler, 12 oz., ftd. iced tea	11.00	20.00	25.00	30.00	
Tumbler, 12 oz., iced tea	11.00	20.00	25.00	30.00	

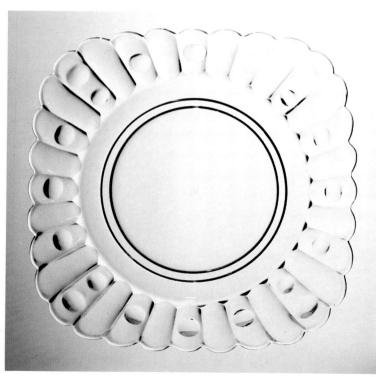

ORCHID (Etching 1507) ON WAVERLY BLANK 11519, A.H. Heisey & Co. 1940-1957

Colors: Crystal

Heisey Orchid has been one of the two top selling patterns of Heisey since the issuance of the first Elegant book. Along with Rose dealers are finding it difficult to keep up with collecting demand especially for hard to find pieces. All listings below are for the WAVERLY blank unless noted. The prices for #5022 GRACEFUL and #5025 TYROLEAN stems have about equaled out so that these are now priced together.

Please note that there are numerous blanks that carry the Orchid etching and many of these items will not be marked. In fact, there is less Orchid marked than there is unmarked, so don't miss a bargain or fail to purchase something you need just because it does not carry the well known diamond "H". Learn to recognize the pattern and you won't go wrong.

	Crystal		Crystal
Ash tray, 3″	22.50	Bowl, 11″, ftd. floral	75.00
Basket, 8½″, LARIAT, ftd.	300.00	Bowl, 12″, crimped floral	60.00
Bell, dinner, #5022 or #5025	115.00	Bowl, 13″, floral	65.00
Bottle, 8 oz., French dressings	135.00	Bowl, 13″, crimped floral	60.00
Bowl, finger, #3309 or #5022 or #5025	47.50	Bowl, 13, gardenia	65.00
Bowl, 4½″, nappy QUEEN ANN	35.00	Butter w/cover, ¼ lb. CABOCHON	185.00
Bowl, 5½″, ftd. mint	32.00	Butter w/cover, 6″,	150.00
Bowl, 6″, jelly, 2 hdld.	30.00	Candleholder, 6″, deep epernette	125.00
Bowl, 6″, oval lemon w/cover QUEEN ANN	175.00	Candlestick, 1-lite MERCURY	30.00
Bowl, 6½″, ftd. honey; cheese QUEEN ANN	32.50	Candlestick, 1-lite QUEEN ANN w/prisms	100.00
Bowl, 6½″, ftd. jelly	30.00	Candlestick 2-lite FLAME	100.00
Bowl, 6½″, 2 pt. oval dressings	45.00	Candlestick, 2 lite 5″, TRIDENT	55.00
Bowl, 7″, lily	40.00	Candlestick 3 lite CASCADE	67.50
Bowl, 7″ salad	42.50	Candlestick, 3 lite WAVERLY	87.50
Bowl, 7″, 3 pt., rnd, relish	42.50	Candy box w/cover, 6″, low ft.	135.00
Bowl, 7″, ftd. honey; cheese	45.00	Candy w/cover, 5″, high ft.	155.00
Bowl, 7″, ftd. jelly	40.00	Candy w/cover, 6″, bow knot finial	150.00
Bowl, 7″, ftd. oval nut	45.00	Cheese (comport) & cracker (11½″) plate	95.00
Bowl, 8″, mint, ftd. QUEEN ANN	55.00	Cheese & cracker, 14″ plate	125.00
Bowl, 8″, nappy, QUEEN ANN	47.50	Chocolate w/cover, 5″	150.00
Bowl, 8″, 2 pt. oval dressings	45.00	Cigarette box w/cover, 4″ PURITAN	100.00
Bowl, 8″, pt., rnd. relish	57.50	Cigarette holder #4035	57.50
Bowl, 8½″, flared, QUEEN ANN	50.00	Cigarette holder w/cover	125.00
Bowl, 8½″, floral, 2 hdld., ftd. QUEEN ANN	57.50	Cocktail icer w/liner UNIVERSAL #3304	85.00
Bowl, 9″, 4 pt., rnd. relish	60.00	Cocktail shaker, pt., #4225	150.00
Bowl, 9″, ft. fruit or salad	75.00	Cocktail shaker, qt. #4036 or #4225	195.00
Bowl, 9″, gardenia QUEEN ANN	50.00	Comport, 5½″ blown	87.50
Bowl, 9″, salad	57.50	Comport, 6″, low ft.	40.00
Bowl, 9½″, crimped floral	47.50	Comport, 6½″, low ft	42.50
Bowl, 9½″, epergne	325.00	Comport, 7″, ftd. oval	95.00
Bowl, 10″, crimped	60.00	Creamer, indiv.	30.00
Bowl, 10″, gardenia	65.00	Creamer, ftd.	27.50
Bowl, 10½″, ftd. floral	75.00	Cup, Waverly or QUEEN ANN	45.00
Bowl, 11″, shallow, rolled edge	67.50	Decanter, oval sherry, pt.	150.00
Bowl, 11″, 3 ftd. floral, seahorse ft.	110.00	Decanter, pt., ftd. #4036	250.00
Bowl, 11″, 3 pt., oblong relish	67.50	Decanter, pt. #4036½	175.00
Bowl, 11″, 4 ftd., oval	75.00	Ice bucket, ftd. QUEEN ANN	165.00
Bowl, 11″, flared	55.00	Ice bucket, 2 hand.	150.00
Bowl, 11″, floral	55.00	Marmalade w/cover	85.00

ORCHID, (Etching 1507) on Waverly Blank 11519, A.H. Heisey & Co., 1940-1957

	Crystal
Mayonnaise, 5½", 1 hand.	40.00
Mayonnaise, 5½", ftd.	40.00
Mayonnaise, 5½", 1 hand., div.	42.50
Mayonnaise, 6½", 1 hand.	50.00
Mayonnaise, 6½", 1 hand., div	52.50
Mustard w/cover QUEEN ANN	125.00
Oil, 3 oz., ftd.	145.00
Pitcher, 73 oz.	325.00
Pitcher, 64 oz. ice tankard	450.00
Plate, 6"	12.50
Plate, 7", mayonnaise	15.00
Plate, 7", salad	15.50
Plate, 8", salad	22.00
Plate, 10½", dinner	85.00
Plate, 11", demi-torte	50.00
Plate, 11", sandwich	50.00
Plate, 12", ftd. salver	200.00
Plate, 13½", ftd. cake or salver	250.00
Plate, 14", torte, rolled edge	52.50
Plate, 14", torte	50.00
Plate, 14", sandwich	80.00
Salt & pepper, pr.	60.00
Salt & pepper, ft., pr.	65.00
Saucer, WAVERLY OR QUEEN ANN	9.00
Stem, #5022 or #5025, 1 oz., cordial	135.00

	Crystal
Stem, #5022 or #5025, 2 oz., sherry	85.00
Stem, #5022 or #5025, 3 oz., wine	60.00
Stem, #5022 or #5025, 4 oz., oyster cocktail	37.50
Stem, #5022 or #5025, 4 oz., cocktail	40.00
Stem, #5022 or #5025, 4½ oz., claret	50.00
Stem, #5022 or #5025, 6 oz., saucer champagne	30.00
Stem, #5022 or #5025, 6 oz., sherbet	25.00
Stem, #5022 or #5025, 10 oz., low water goblet	35.00
Stem, #5022 or #5025, 10 oz., water goblet	40.00
Sugar, indiv.	30.00
Sugar, ftd.	27.50
Toast w/dome	145.00
Tray, 12", celery	45.00
Tray, 13", celery	47.50
Tumbler, #5022 or #5025, 5 oz. fruit	35.00
Tumbler, #5022 or #5025, 12 oz., iced tea	57.50
Vase, 4", ftd. violet	67.50
Vase, 6", crimped top	95.00
Vase, 7", ftd. fan	75.00
Vase, 7", ftd.	72.50
Vase, 8", ftd. bud	125.00
Vase, 8", sq. ftd. bud	125.00
Vase, 10". sq. ftd. bud	110.00

PLANTATION, Blank # 1567, A. H. Heisey & Co.

Colors: crystal; rare in amber

	Crystal		Crystal
Ash tray, 3½″	17.50	Marmadale w/cover	50.00
Bowl, 9 qt. Dr. Johnson punch	250.00	Mayonnaise, 4½″, rolled ft.	45.00
Bowl, 5″, nappy	13.00	Mayonnaise, 5¼″, w/liner	22.00
Bowl, 5½″, nappy	14.00	Oil bottle, 3 oz., w/#125 stopper	50.00
Bowl, 6½″, 2 hdld. jelly	17.50	Pitcher, ½ gallon, ice lip, blown	95.00
Bowl, 6½″, flared jelly	18.00	Plate, coupe (rare)	150.00
Bowl, 6½″, ftd. honey, cupped	25.00	Plate, 7″, salad	10.00
Bowl, 8″, 4 pt., rnd. relish	25.00	Plate, 8″, salad	12.00
Bowl, 8½″, 2 pt., dressing	18.00	Plate, 10½″, demi-torte	20.00
Bowl, 9″, salad	25.00	Plate, 13″, ftd. cake salver	80.00
Bowl, 9½″, crimped, fruit or flower	25.00	Plate, 14″, sandwich	35.00
Bowl, 9½″, gardenia	25.00	Plate, 18″, buffet	40.00
Bowl, 11″, 3 part relish	22.50	Plate, 18″, punch bowl liner	80.00
Bowl, 11½″, ftd. gardenia	30.00	Salt & pepper, pr	30.00
Bowl, 12″, crimped, fruit or flower	35.00	Saucer	5.00
Bowl, 13″, celery	20.00	Stem, 1 oz., cordial	75.00
Bowl, 13″, 2 part celery	25.00	Stem, 3 oz., wine, blown	30.00
Bowl, 13″, 5 part oval relish	35.00	Stem, 3½ oz., cocktail, pressed	20.00
Bowl, 13″, gardenia	30.00	Stem, 4 oz., fruit/oyster cocktail	15.00
Butter, ¼ lb., oblong w/cover	50.00	Stem, 4½ oz., claret, blown	20.00
Butter, 5″, rnd. (or cov. candy)	60.00	Stem, 4½ oz., claret, pressed	20.00
Candelabrum w/two #1503 bobeche		Stem, 4½ oz., oyster cocktail, blown	18.00
and ten "A" prisms	32.50	Stem, 6½ oz., sherbet/saucer	
Candle block, hurricane type	85.00	champagne, blown	18.00
Candle block, 1-lite	65.00	Stem, 10 oz., pressed	17.00
Candle holder, 5″, ftd. epergne	40.00	Stem, 10 oz., blown	17.00
Candlestick, 1-lite	60.00	Sugar, ftd.	15.00
Candlestick, 2-lite	32.00	Syrup bottle w/drip, cut top	50.00
Candlestick, 3-lite	65.00	Tray, 8½″, condiment/sugar &	
Candy box w/cover, 7″	95.00	creamer	20.00
Candy w/cover, 5″, tall, ftd.	125.00	Tumbler, 5 oz., ftd. juice, pressed	22.50
Cheese w/cover, 5″, ftd.	65.00	Tumbler, 5 oz., ftd. juice, blown	25.00
Coaster, 4″	12.00	Tumbler, 10 oz., pressed	27.50
Comport, 5″	20.00	Tumbler, 12 oz., ftd. iced tea, pressed	26.00
Comport, 5″, w/cover, deep	45.00	Tumbler, 12 oz., ftd. iced tea, blown	28.00
Creamer, ftd.	15.00	Vase, 5″, ftd., flared	30.00
Cup	12.00	Vase, 9″, ftd., flared	35.00
Cup, punch	20.00		

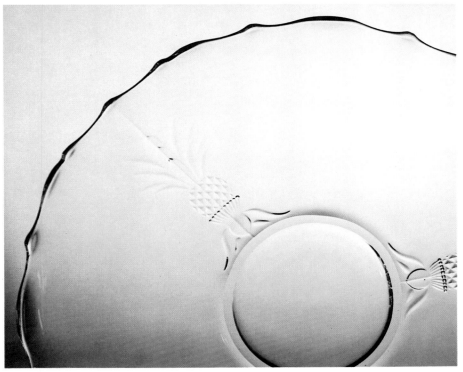

PORTIA, Cambridge Glass Company, 1932 - Early 1950's

Colors: crystal, yellow, Heatherbloom, green

	Crystal		Crystal
Basket, 2 hdld. (upturned sides)	16.00	Set: 3 pc. Frappe (bowl, 2 plain inserts)	22.50
Basket, 7", 1 hdld	100.00	Stem, #3121, 1 oz., cordial	50.00
Bowl, 3½", cranberry	15.00	Stem, #3121, 1 oz., low ftd. brandy	30.00
Bowl, 3½", sq. cranberry	12.50	Stem, #3121, 2½ oz., wine	22.50
Bowl, 5¼", 2 hdld. bonbon	15.00	Stem, #3121, 3 oz., cocktail	20.00
Bowl, 6", 2 pt. relish	16.00	Stem, #3121, 4½ oz. claret	22.50
Bowl, 6", ftd., 2 hdld. bonbon	16.00	Stem, #3121, 4½ oz., oyster cocktail	15.00
Bowl, 6", grapefruit or oyster	12.00	Stem, #3121, 5 oz., parfait	20.00
Bowl, 6½", 3 pt. relish	15.00	Stem, #3121, 6 oz., low sherbet	13.00
Bowl, 7", 2 pt. relish	16.00	Stem, #3121, 6 oz., tall sherbet	15.00
Bowl, 7", ftd. bonbon, tab hdld.	20.00	Stem, #3121, 10 oz. goblet	20.00
Bowl, 7", pickle or relish	18.00	Stem, #3124, 3 oz., cocktail	15.00
Bowl, 9", 3 pt. celery & relish, tab hdld.	22.50	Stem, #3124, 3 oz., wine	20.00
Bowl, 9½", ftd. pickle (like corn bowl)	20.00	Stem, #3124, 4½ oz., claret	18.00
Bowl, 10", flared, 4 ftd.	30.00	Stem, #3124, 7 oz., low sherbet	14.00
Bowl, 11", 2 pt., 2 hdld. "figure 8" relish	27.50	Stem, #3124, 7 oz., tall sherbet	15.00
Bowl, 11", 2 hdld.	25.00	Stem, #3124, 10 oz., goblet	18.00
Bowl, 12", 3 pt. celery & relish, tab hdld.	30.00	Stem, #3126, 1 oz., cordial	45.00
Bowl, 12", 5 pt. celery & relish	32.50	Stem, #3126, 1 oz., low ft. brandy	30.00
Bowl, 12", flared, 4 ftd.	30.00	Stem, #3126, 2½ oz., wine	22.50
Bowl, 12", oval, 4 ftd., "ears" handles	37.50	Stem, #3126, 3 oz., cocktail	17.50
Bowl, finger w/liner #3124	20.00	Stem, #3126, 4½ oz., claret	22.50
Bowl, seafood (fruit cocktail w/liner)	15.00	Stem, #3126, 4½ oz., low ft. oyster cocktail	12.50
Candlestick, 5"	17.50	Stem, #3126, 7 oz., low sherbet	14.00
Candlestick, 6", 2-lite, "fleur de lis"	25.00	Stem, #3126, 7 oz., tall sherbet	15.00
Candlestick, 6", 3-lite	35.00	Stem, #3126, 9 oz., goblet	18.00
Candy box w/cover, rnd.	50.00	Stem, #3130, 1 oz., cordial	50.00
Cigarette holder, urn shape	37.50	Stem, #3130, 2½ oz., wine	22.50
Cocktail icer, 2 pt.	32.50	Stem, #3130, 3 oz., cocktail	17.50
Cocktail shaker w/stopper	65.00	Stem, #3130, 4½ oz., claret	22.50
Cocktail shaker, 80 oz., hdld. ball w/chrome		Stem, fruit/oyster cocktail, #3130, 4½ oz.	15.00
top	75.00	Stem, #3130, 7 oz., low sherbet	14.00
Cologne, 2 oz., hdld. ball w/stopper	32.50	Stem, #3130, 7 oz., tall sherbet	15.00
Comport, 5½"	27.50	Stem, #3130, 9 oz., goblet	20.00
Comport, 5⅜", blown	35.00	Sugar, ftd. hdld. ball	14.00
Creamer, hdld. ball	15.00	Sugar, indiv.	11.50
Creamer, indiv.	11.50	Tray, 11", celery	22.50
Cup, ftd. sq.	18.00	Tumbler, #3121, 2½ oz. bar	17.50
Decanter, 29 oz. ftd. sherry w/stopper	100.00	Tumbler, #3121, 5 oz., ftd. juice	15.00
Hurricane lamp, candlestick base	110.00	Tumbler, #3121, 10 oz., ftd. water	16.50
Hurricane lamp, keyhole base w/prisms	90.00	Tumbler, #3121, 12 oz., ftd. tea	20.00
Ice bucket w/chrome handle	55.00	Tumbler, #3124, 3 oz.	12.50
Ivy ball, 5¼"	25.00	Tumbler, #3124, 5 oz., juice	12.50
Mayonnaise, div. bowl w/liner and 2 ladles	35.00	Tumbler, #3124, 10 oz., water	15.00
Mayonnaise w/liner and ladle	30.00	Tumbler, #3124, 12 oz., tea	15.00
Oil, 6 oz., loop hdld. w/stopper	45.00	Tumbler, #3126, 2½ oz.	17.50
Oil, 6 oz., hdld. ball w/stopper	50.00	Tumbler, #3126, 5 oz., juice	14.00
Pitcher, ball	100.00	Tumbler, #3126, 10 oz., water	15.00
Pitcher, Doulton	175.00	Tumbler, #3126, 12 oz., tea	15.00
Plate, 6", 2 hdld.	15.00	Tumbler, #3130, 5 oz., juice	15.00
Plate, 6½", bread/butter	7.50	Tumbler, #3130, 10 oz., water	15.00
Plate, 8", salad	12.50	Tumbler, #3130, 12 oz., tea	17.50
Plate, 8", ftd. 2 hdld.	17.50	Tumbler, 13 oz., "roly-poly"	15.00
Plate, 8", ftd. bonbon, tab hdld.	20.00	Vase, 5", globe	27.50
Plate, 8½", sq.	15.00	Vase, 6", ftd.	27.50
Plate, 10½", dinner	35.00	Vase, 8", ftd.	30.00
Plate, 13", 4 ftd. torte	30.00	Vase, 9", keyhole ft.	37.50
Plate, 13½", 2 hdld. cake	27.50	Vase, 10", bud	25.00
Plate, 14", torte	35.00	Vase, 11", flower	35.00
Puff box, 3½", ball shape w/lid	45.00	Vase, 11", pedestal ft.	35.00
Salt & pepper, pr.	25.00	Vase, 12", keyhole ft.	50.00
Saucer, sq. or rnd.	3.00	Vase, 13", flower	65.00

Note: See Pages 148-149 for stem identification.

PROVINCIAL, Blank #1506, A. H. Heisey & Co.

Colors: crystal, "Limelight" green

	Crystal	Green
Ash tray, 3″ square	12.00	
Bonbon dish, 7″, 2 hdld., upturned sides	10.00	35.00
Bowl, 5 quart punch	60.00	
Bowl, individual nut/jelly	20.00	25.00
Bowl, 4½″, nappy	10.00	27.50
Bowl, 5″, 2 hdld. nut/jelly	12.00	
Bowl, 5½″, nappy	12.00	35.00
Bowl, 5½″, round, hdld. nappy	15.00	50.00
Bowl, 5½″, tri-corner, hdld. nappy	17.00	50.00
Bowl, 10″, 4 part relish	32.50	175.00
Bowl, 12″, floral	32.50	
Bowl, 13″, gardenia	32.50	
Box, 5½″, footed candy w/cover	85.00	300.00
Butter dish w/cover	70.00	
Candle, 1-lite, block	17.00	
Candle, 3-lite	37.50	
Candle, 3-lite, #4233 5″, vase	50.00	
Cigarette lighter	25.00	
Coaster, 4″	5.00	
Creamer, footed	15.00	85.00
Creamer & sugar w/tray, individual	35.00	
Cup, punch	10.00	
Mayonnaise, 7″ (plate, ladle, bowl)	30.00	135.00
Oil bottle, 4 oz., #1 stopper	40.00	
Plate, 5″, footed cheese	10.00	
Plate, 7″, 2 hdld. snack	12.00	
Plate, 7″, bread	10.00	
Plate, 8″, luncheon	15.00	40.00
Plate, 14″, torte	25.00	
Plate, 18″, buffet	35.00	150.00
Salt & Pepper, pr	20.00	
Stem, 3½ oz., oyster cocktail	8.00	
Stem, 3½ oz., wine	17.50	
Stem, 5 oz., sherbet/champagne	8.00	
Stem, 10 oz.	17.50	
Sugar, footed	15.00	80.00
Tray, 13″, oval celery	20.00	
Tumbler, 5 oz., footed juice	10.00	35.00
Tumbler, 8 oz.,	12.00	
Tumbler, 9 oz., footed	14.00	60.00
Tumbler, 12 oz., footed, iced tea	15.00	70.00
Tumbler, 13″, flat ice tea	15.00	
Vase, 3½″, violet	15.00	70.00
Vase, 4″, pansy	15.00	
Vase, 6″, sweet pea	20.00	

RIDGELEIGH, Blank #1469, A. H. Heisey & Co.

Colors: crystal, "Sahara," "Zircon," rare

	Crystal		Crystal
Ash tray, round	4.00	Mustard w/cover	30.00
Ash tray, square	3.00	Oil bottle, 3 oz., w/#103 stopper	40.00
Ash tray, 4", round	10.00	Pitcher, ½ gallon	75.00
Ash tray, 6", square	15.00	Pitcher, ½ gallon, ice lip	85.00
Ash trays, bridge set (heart, diamond, spade,		Plate, oval hors d'oeuvres	20.00
club)	27.50	Plate, 2 hdld. ice tub liner	15.00
Basket, bonbon	9.00	Plate, 6", round	5.00
Bottle, rock & rye w/#104 stopper	80.00	Plate, 6", scalloped	5.00
Bottle, 4 oz., cologne	45.00	Plate, 6", square	5.00
Bottle, 5 oz., bitters w/tube	50.00	Plate, 7", square	6.00
Bowl, indiv. nut	7.00	Plate, 8", round	7.00
Bowl, oval indiv. jelly	12.00	Plate, 8", square	7.00
Bowl, indiv. nut, 2 part	10.00	Plate, 13½", sandwich	20.00
Bowl, 4½", nappy, bell or cupped	6.00	Plate, 13½", ftd. torte	20.00
Bowl, 4½", nappy, scalloped	6.00	Plate, 14", salver	50.00
Bowl, 5", lemon w/cover	15.00	Salt & pepper, pr.	22.50
Bowl, 5", nappy, straight	6.00	Salt dip, indiv.	12.50
Bowl, 5", nappy, square	6.00	Saucer	3.00
Bowl, 6", 2 hdld. divided jelly	12.50	Soda, 12 oz., cupped or flared	22.00
Bowl, 6", 2 hdld. jelly	12.50	Stem, cocktail, pressed	17.50
Bowl, 7", 2 part oval relish	12.50	Stem, claret, pressed	22.50
Bowl, 8", centerpiece	20.00	Stem, oyster cocktail, pressed	12.00
Bowl, 8", nappy, square	25.00	Stem, sherbet, pressed	8.00
Bowl, 9", nappy, square	25.00	Stem, saucer champagne, pressed	10.00
Bowl, 9", salad	27.50	Stem, wine, pressed	22.50
Bowl, 10", flared fruit	30.00	Stem, 1 oz., cordial, blown	100.00
Bowl, 10", floral	30.00	Stem, 2 oz., sherry, blown	50.00
Bowl, 11", centerpiece	32.50	Stem, 2½ oz., wine, blown	45.00
Bowl, 11", punch	65.00	Stem, 3½ oz., cocktail blown	26.00
Bowl, 11½", floral	27.50	Stem, 4 oz., claret, blown	27.50
Bowl, 12", oval floral	32.00	Stem, 4 oz., oyster cocktail, blown	16.00
Bowl, 12", flared fruit	32.00	Stem, 5 oz., saucer champagne, blown	17.50
Bowl, 13", cone floral	32.00	Stem, 5 oz., sherbet, blown	12.50
Bowl, 14", oblong floral	40.00	Stem, 8 oz., luncheon, low stem	12.50
Bowl, 14", oblong swan hdld. floral	75.00	Stem, 8 oz., tall stem	17.50
Box, 8", floral	20.00	Sugar	15.00
Candle block, 3"	15.00	Sugar, indiv.	10.00
Candle vase, 6"	15.00	Tray, for indiv. sugar & creamer	10.00
Candlestick, 2", 1-lite	10.00	Tray, 10½", oblong	20.00
Candlestick, 2-lite, bobeche & "A" prisms	30.00	Tray, 11", 3 part, relish	25.00
Candlestick, 7", w/bobeche & "A" prisms	75.00	Tray, 12", celery & olive, divided	22.00
Cheese, 6", 2 hdld.	7.00	Tray, 12", celery	20.00
Cigarette box w/cover, oval	25.00	Tumbler, 2½ oz., bar, pressed	15.00
Cigarette box w/cover, 6"	10.00	Tumbler, 5 oz., juice, blown	15.00
Cigarette holder, oval w/2 comp. ash trays	35.00	Tumbler, 5 oz., soda, ftd., pressed	12.00
Cigarette holder, round	6.00	Tumbler, 8 oz., (#1469¾), pressed	14.00
Cigarette holder, square	6.00	Tumbler, 8 oz., old fashioned, pressed	15.00
Cigarette holder w/cover	15.00	Tumbler, 8 oz., soda, blown	15.00
Coaster or cocktail rest	3.00	Tumbler, 10 oz., (#1469¾), pressed	12.00
Cocktail shaker, 1 qt. w/#1 strainer & #86 stopper	100.00	Tumbler, 12 oz., ftd. soda, pressed	17.00
Comport, 6", low ft., flared	15.00	Tumbler, 12 oz., soda, (#1469¾) pressed	22.00
Comport, 6", low ft. w/cover	25.00	Tumbler, 13 oz., iced tea, blown	15.00
Creamer	15.00	Vase, #1 indiv., cuspidor shape	22.50
Creamer, indiv.	10.00	Vase, #2 indiv., cupped top	21.00
Cup	10.00	Vase, #3 indiv., flared rim	22.50
Cup, beverage	12.00	Vase, #4, indiv., fan out top	25.00
Cup, punch	10.00	Vase, #5 indiv., scalloped top	22.50
Decanter, 1 pint w/#95 stopper	70.00	Vase, 3½"	20.00
Ice tub, 2 hdld.	35.00	Vase, 6", (also flared)	15.00
Marmalade w/cover	32.50	Vase, 8"	20.00
Mayonnaise	25.00	Vase, 8", triangular (#1469¾)	20.00

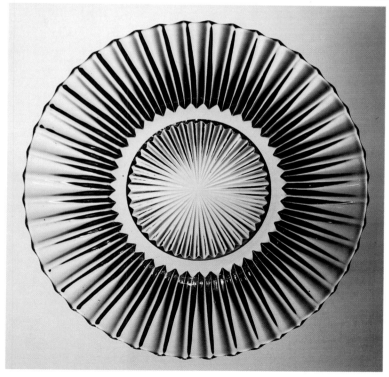

ROSALIE, or #731, Cambridge Glass Company, Late 1920's - 1930's

Colors: blue, green, Heatherbloom, pink

A special thanks to Lynn Welker for letting me know that #731 had a much prettier name . . . ROSALIE. It is easier for collectors to refer to a name for a pattern than just a company number.

Prices listed below will hold for all colors except the blue and Heatherbloom which will be 10% to 20% more.

	All Colors		All Colors
Bottle, French dressing	45.00	Cup	12.50
Bowl, bouillon, 2 hdld.	15.00	Gravy, double, w/platter	75.00
Bowl, cream soup	17.50	Ice bucket or pail	37.50
Bowl, finger, w/liner	20.00	Ice tub	35.00
Bowl, finger, ftd., w/liner	22.50	Mayonnaise, ftd. w/liner	30.00
Bowl, 3½″, cranberry	12.50	Nut, 2½″, ftd.	22.50
Bowl, 3⅝″, w/cover, 3 pt.	22.50	Pitcher, 62 oz., #955	97.50
Bowl, 5½″, fruit	12.50	Plate, 6¾″, bread/butter	5.50
Bowl, 5½″, 2 hdld., bonbon	15.00	Plate, 7″, 2 hdld.	12.50
Bowl, 6¼″, 2 hdld., bonbon	17.50	Plate, 7½″, salad	8.50
Bowl, 7″, basket, 2 hdld.	200.00	Plate, 8⅜″	13.50
Bowl, 8½″, soup	22.50	Plate, 9½″, dinner	25.00
Bowl, 8½″, 2 hdld.	20.00	Plate, 11″, 2 hdld.	22.50
Bowl, 8½″, w/cover, 3 pt.	32.50	Platter, 12″	30.00
Bowl, 10″	25.00	Platter, 15″	42.50
Bowl, 10″, 2 hdld.	27.50	Relish, 9″, 2 pt.	17.50
Bowl, 11″	30.00	Relish, 11″, 2 pt.	25.00
Bowl, 11″, basket, 2 hdld.	37.50	Salt dip, 1½″, ftd.	12.50
Bowl, 11½″	32.50	Saucer	2.50
Bowl, 12″	32.50	Stem, 1 oz., cordial #3077	37.50
Bowl, 13″, console	32.50	Stem, 3½ oz., cocktail #3077	17.50
Bowl, 15″, oval console	35.00	Stem, 6 oz., low sherbet, #3077	13.50
Bowl, 15″, oval, flanged	40.00	Stem, 6 oz., high sherbet, #3077	15.00
Bowl, 15½″, oval	37.50	Stem, 9 oz., water goblet, #3077	22.50
Candlestick, 4″, 2 styles	15.00	Stem, 10 oz., goblet #801	22.50
Candlestick, 5″, keyhole	17.50	Sugar, ftd.	12.00
Candlestick, 6″, 3-lite keyhole	25.00	Sugar shaker	75.00
Candy and cover, 6″	57.50	Tray for sugar shaker/creamer	17.50
Celery, 11″	22.50	Tray, ctr. hdld., for sugar/creamer	15.00
Cheese & cracker, 11″ plate	37.50	Tray, 11″, ctr. hdld.	30.00
Comport, 5½″, 2 hdld.	20.00	Tumbler, 2½ oz., ftd., #3077	13.50
Comport, 5¾″	17.50	Tumbler, 5 oz., ftd., #3077	15.00
Comport, 6″, ftd. almond	30.00	Tumbler, 8 oz., ftd., #3077	15.00
Comport, 6½″, low ft.	20.00	Tumbler, 10 oz., ftd., #3077	17.50
Comport, 6½″, high ft.	25.00	Tumbler, 12 oz., ftd., #3077	20.00
Comport, 6¾″	22.50	Vase, 5½″, ftd.	35.00
Creamer, ftd.	12.50	Vase, 6″	40.00
Creamer, ftd., tall	20.00	Vase, 6½″, ftd.	42.50

ROSE, Etching #1515, on WAVERLY Blank #11519, A. H. Heisey & Co., 1949 - 1957

Colors: crystal

Rose, one of the loveliest of Heisey patterns, is very collectible today. Notice that the stems are thorny rose bud designs! Some items of this pattern were taken over and manufactured by Imperial Glass Company after Heisey ceased operation in 1957.

Notice the 6″ deep epernette on the 3 lite candlestick in the top picture. It is very rare!

Item	Crystal	Item	Crystal
Ash tray, 3″	40.00	Cocktail icer w/liner, #3304, UNIVERSAL	50.00
Bell, dinner #5072	110.00	Cocktail shaker, #4036 & #4225, COBEL	70.00
Bottle, 8 oz., French dressing, blown, #5031	165.00	Comport, 6½″, low ft., WAVERLY	60.00
Bowl, finger, #3309	50.00	Comport, 7″, oval, ftd., WAVERLY	100.00
Bowl, 5½″, ftd. mint	32.50	Creamer, ftd., WAVERLY	32.50
Bowl, 5¾″, ftd. mint. CABOCHON	67.50	Creamer, indiv., WAVERLY	25.00
Bowl, 6″, ftd. mint, QUEEN ANN	37.50	Cup, WAVERLY	50.00
Bowl, 6″, jelly, 2 hdld., ftd. QUEEN ANN	42.50	Decanter, 1 pt., #4036½, #101 stopper	100.00
Bowl, 6″, oval lemon w/cover	147.50	Hurricane lamp w/12″ globe #5080	125.00
Bowl, 6½″, 2 pt. oval dressing, WAVERLY	55.00	Hurricane lamp, w/12″ globe, PLANTATION	125.00
Bowl, 6½″, ftd. honey/cheese, WAVERLY	50.00	Ice bucket, dolp. ft., QUEEN ANN	150.00
Bowl, 6½″, ftd. jelly, WAVERLY	45.00	Ice tub, 2 hdld., WAVERLY	150.00
Bowl, 6½″, lemon w/cover, WAVERLY	147.50	Mayonnaise, 5½″, 2 hdld., WAVERLY	50.00
Bowl, 7″, ftd. honey, WAVERLY	40.00	Mayonnaise, 5½″, div., 1 hdld., WAVERLY	50.00
Bowl, 7″, ftd. jelly, WAVERLY	40.00	Mayonnaise, 5½″, ftd., WAVERLY	55.00
Bowl, 7″, lily, QUEEN ANN	45.00	Oil, 3 oz., ftd., WAVERLY	145.00
Bowl, 7″, relish, 3 pt., round, WAVERLY	67.50	Pitcher, 73 oz., #4164	225.00
Bowl, 7″, salad, WAVERLY	52.50	Plate, 7″, salad, WAVERLY	20.00
Bowl, 7″, salad dressings, QUEEN ANN	50.00	Plate, 7″, mayonnaise, WAVERLY	20.00
Bowl, 9″, ftd. fruit or salad, WAVERLY	90.00	Plate, 8″, salad, WAVERLY	30.00
Bowl, 9″, salad, WAVERLY	75.00	Plate, 10½″, dinner	85.00
Bowl, 9″, 4 pt. rnd. relish, WAVERLY	75.00	Plate, 10½″, service, WAVERLY	75.00
Bowl, 9½″, crimped floral, WAVERLY	65.00	Plate, 11″, sandwich, WAVERLY	75.00
Bowl, 10″, gardenia, WAVERLY	65.00	Plate, 11″, demi-torte, WAVERLY	65.00
Bowl, 10″, crimped floral, WAVERLY	82.50	Plate, 12″, ftd. salver, WAVERLY	150.00
Bowl, 11″, 3 pt. relish, WAVERLY	77.50	Plate, 15″, ftd. cake, WAVERLY	225.00
Bowl, 11″, 3 ft., floral, WAVERLY	115.00	Plate, 14″, torte, WAVERLY	90.00
Bowl, 11″, floral, WAVERLY	67.50	Plate, 14″, sandwich, WAVERLY	90.00
Bowl, 11″, oval, 4 ft., WAVERLY	110.00	Plate, 14″, ctr. hdld., sandwich, WAVERLY	150.00
Bowl, 12″, crimped floral, WAVERLY	75.00	Salt & pepper, ftd., pr., WAVERLY	65.00
Bowl, 13″, crimped floral, WAVERLY	80.00	Saucer, WAVERLY	10.00
Bowl, 13″, floral, WAVERLY	80.00	Stem, #5072, 1 oz., cordial	135.00
Bowl, 13″, gardenia, WAVERLY	75.00	Stem, #5072, 3 oz., wine	100.00
Butter w/cover, 6″,. WAVERLY	150.00	Stem, #5072, 3½ oz., oyster cocktail, ftd.	27.50
Butter w/cover, ¼ lb., CABOCHON	175.00	Stem, #5072, 4 oz., claret	90.00
Candlestick, 1-lite, #112	35.00	Stem, #5072, 4 oz., cocktail	40.00
Candlestick, 2-lite, FLAME	45.00	Stem, #5072, 6 oz., sherbet	27.50
Candlestick, 3-lite, #142 CASCADE	77.50	Stem, #5072, 6 oz., saucer champagne	35.00
Candlestick, 3-lite, WAVERLY	80.00	Stem, #5072, 9 oz., water	42.50
Candlestick, 5″, 2-lite, #134, TRIDENT	45.00	Sugar, indiv., WAVERLY	25.00
Candlestick, 6″, epergnette, deep, WAVERLY	150.00	Sugar, ftd., WAVERLY	30.00
Candy w/cover, 5″, ftd. WAVERLY	140.00	Tumbler, #5072, 5 oz., ftd. juice	42.50
Candy w/cover, 6″, low, bowknot cover	150.00	Tumbler, #5072, 12 oz., ftd. tea	45.00
Candy w/cover, 6¼″, #1951, CABOCHON	95.00	Tray, indiv. creamer/sugar, QUEEN ANN	25.00
Celery tray, 12″, WAVERLY	45.00	Vase, 3½″, ftd. violet, WAVERLY	52.50
Celery tray, 13″, WAVERLY	50.00	Vase, 4″, ftd. violet, WAVERLY	55.00
Cheese compote, 4½″, & cracker (11″ plate) WAVERLY	75.00	Vase, 7″, ftd. fan, WAVERLY	57.50
Cheese compote, 5½″, & cracker (12″ plate) QUEEN ANNE	75.00	Vase, 8″, #4198	75.00
Chocolate w/cover, 5″, WAVERLY	90.00	Vase, 8″, sq. ftd. urn	60.00
Cigarette holder, #4035	75.00	Vase, 10″, #4198	100.00
		Vase, 10″, sq. ftd. urn	75.00
		Vase, 12″, sq. fd. urn	125.00

ROSE POINT, Cambridge Glass Company, 1936 - 1953

Colors: crystal, some crystal with gold

Rose Point has become the most collected Cambridge pattern. You may note that not all pieces you may find are in my listing since almost any blank that Cambridge made could turn up with Rose Point etching. As time goes by, little by little, we'll get as much as possible listed. Now, you will usually find only one line listed on such items as plates. There are as many as three lines on many items; but since almost all items are priced in the same range, for now I will show one size and not each line. One problem I have run up against this time was an unwillingness among some Cambridge collectors to relinquish information for publication. This is an obstacle that I will overcome in time, but unfortunately for you, not in time for this publication.

If you have any catalog information available to you on any patterns in this book, please contact me. Contrary to some beliefs, information given freely to the public saves more of our precious glass from destruction than any other source.

	Crystal
Ash tray, 2½", sq.	35.00
Ash tray, 3¼" (#3500/124)	30.00
Ash tray, 3½" (#3500/125)	31.50
Ash tray, 4" (#3500/126)	32.50
Ash tray, 4¼" (#3500/127)	33.50
Ashtray, 4½" (#3500/128)	35.00
Basket, 5", 1 hdld. (#3500/51)	150.00
Basket, 6", 1 hdld. (#3500/52)	165.00
Basket, 7", 1 hdld.	285.00
Bowl, 3", 4 ftd. nut (#3400/71)	40.00
Bowl, 5", hdld. (#3500/49)	39.50
Bowl, 5¼", 2 hdld. bonbon (#3400/1180)	30.00
Bowl, 5½" nappy (#3400/56)	32.50
Bowl, 6", cereal (#3500/11)	37.50
Bowl, 6", hdld. (#3500/50)	40.00
Bowl, 6", 2 hdld. ftd. basket (#3500/55)	35.00
Bowl, 6", 2 hdld. ftd. bonbon (#3500/54)	30.00
Bowl, 6", 2 pt. relish (#3400/90)	30.00
Bowl, 6½", 3 pt. relish (#3500/69)	30.00
Bowl, 7", 2 pt relish (#3900/124)	32.50
Bowl, 7", relish (#3900/123)	32.50
Bowl, 7", tab hdld. ftd. bonbon (#3900/130)	32.50
Bowl, 8", 3 pt. relish (#3400/91)	37.50
Bowl, 8", 3 pt., 3 hdld. relish (#3400/91)	42.50
Bowl, 8½", soup	50.00
Bowl, 9", 3 pt. celery & relish (#3900/125)	40.00
Bowl, 9½", pickle (like corn)	30.00
Bowl, 10", 2 hdld. (#3500/28)	52.50
Bowl, 10", 4 tab ftd., flared (#3900/54)	52.50
Bowl, 10½", flared (#3400/168)	52.50
Bowl, 10½", 3 pt. (#1401/122)	75.00
Bowl, 11", 4 ftd. shallow, fancy edge (#3400/48)	60.00
Bowl, 11", tab hdld. (#3900/48)	52.50
Bowl, 11½", ftd. w/tab hdl. (#3900/28)	57.50
Bowl, 12", 4 ftd., oval w/"ears" hdl. (#3900/65)	72.50
Bowl, 12", 3 pt. celery & relish (#3900/126)	47.50
Bowl, 12", 4 ftd. fancy rim oblong (#3400/160)	67.50
Bowl, 12", 4 ftd. flared (#3400/4)	60.00
Bowl, 12", 4 tab ftd., flared (#3900/62)	62.50
Bowl, 12", 5 pt. celery & relish (#3900/120)	55.00
Butter w/cover, ¼ lb.	265.00
Butter w/cover, 5" (#3400/52)	165.00
Candlestick, 5" (#3900/68)	30.00
Candlestick, 5", 1-lite keyhole (#3400/646)	32.50
Candlestick, 5", inverts to comport (#3900/67)	37.50
Candlestick, 6", 2-lite keyhole (#3400/647)	30.00
Candlestick, 6", 2-lite (#3900/72)	35.00
Candlestick, 6", 3-lite keyhole (#3400/648)	40.00
Candlestick, 6", 3-tiered lite	65.00
Candy box w/cover, 5⅜", #1066 stem	115.00

	Crystal
Candy box w/cover, 6″ ram's head (#3500/78)	150.00
Candy box w/cover, 7″	120.00
Candy box w/cover, 8″, 3 pt. (#3500/57)	67.50
Candy box w/cover, rnd. (#3900/165)	95.00
Cheese (comport) & cracker (13″ plate) (#3900/135)	100.00
Cheese dish w/cover	375.00
Cigarette box w/cover (2 sizes)	90.00
Coaster	35.00
Cocktail icer, 2 pc. (#3600)	67.50
Cocktail shaker, metal top (#3400/175)	135.00
Cocktail shaker, 32 oz., w/stopper	125.00
Comport, 5″, 4 fd. (#3400/74)	32.50
Comport, 5½″, scalloped edge (#3900/136)	37.50
Comport, 5⅜″, blown (#3500/101)	52.50
Comport, 5⅜″, blown #3121 stem	52.50
Comport, 5⅜″, blown #1066 stem	52.50
Creamer, flat	87.50
Creamer, ftd. (#3900/41)	21.50
Creamer, indiv. (#3500/15) pie crust edge	22.50
Creamer, indiv. (#3900/40) scalloped edge	22.50
Cup, 3 styles (#3400, #3500, #3900)	30.00
Decanter, 12 oz., ball, w/stopper (#3400/92)	125.00
Decanter, 28 oz. w/stopper	215.00
Decanter, 32 oz., ball, w/stopper (#3400/92)	150.00
Epergne (candle w/vases) (#3900/75)	135.00
Grapefruit w/liner	75.00
Honey dish w/cover (#3500/139)	195.00
Hurricane lamp w/prisms	195.00
Hurricane lamp, candlestick base	175.00
Hurricane lamp, keyhole base w/prisms	225.00
Ice bucket w/chrome hand. (#3900/671)	125.00
Marmalade, 8 oz.	110.00
Mayonnaise, (sherbet type w/ladle)	50.00
Mayonnaise, div. w/liner & 2 ladles (#3900/111)	75.00
Mayonnaise w/liner & ladle (#3500/59)	60.00
Mustard, 3 oz.	100.00
Oil, 2 oz., ball, w/stopper (#3400/96)	42.50
Oil, 6 oz., ball, w/stopper (#3400/99)	57.50
Oil, 6 oz., loop hdld. w/stopper (#3900/11)	110.00
Oil, 6 oz., w/stopper, ftd., hdld. (#3400/161)	145.00
Pitcher, 20 oz. (#3900/117)	195.00
Pitcher, 32 oz. (#3900/118)	165.00
Pitcher, 32 oz. martini (slender) w/metal insert	450.00
Pitcher, 60 oz. martini	1250.00
Pitcher, 76 oz. (#3900/115)	155.00
Pitcher, 76 oz., ice lip (#3400/152)	165.00
Pitcher, 80 oz., Doulton (#3400/141)	255.00
Pitcher, 80 oz., ball (#3400/80)	155.00
Pitcher, nite set, 2 pc. w/tumbler insert top	325.00
Plate, 6″, 2 hdld. (#3400/1181)	15.00
Plate, 6⅛″ canape	75.00
Plate, 6½″, bread/butter (#3900/20)	12.50
Plate, 7½″, salad (#3400/176)	15.00
Plate, 8″, 2 hdld. ftd. (#3500/161)	25.00
Plate, 8″, tab hdld. ftd. bonbon (#3900/131)	27.50
Plate, 8½″, breakfast (#3400/62)	20.00
Plate 9½″ crescent salad	150.00
Plate, 9½″, luncheon (#3400/63)	30.00
Plate, 10½″, dinner (#3400/64)	105.00
Plate, 11″, 2 hdld. (#3400/35)	55.00
Plate, 12″, 4 ftd. service (#3900/26)	52.50
Plate, 12½″, 2 hdld. (#3400/1186)	57.50
Plate, 13″, rolled edge, ftd. (#3900/33)	65.00

Plate, 13″, 4 ftd. torte (#3500/110)	65.00
Plate, 13½″, rolled edge	72.50
Plate, 13½″, tab hdld. cake (#3900/35)	67.50
Plate, 14″, service (#3900/167)	72.50
Plate, 14″ torte (#3400/65)	72.50
Punch bowl, 15″	1,000.00
Relish, 3 pt., center hdld. (#3500/71)	125.00
Relish, 10″, 4 pt. (#3500/65)	55.00
Relish, 15″, 4 pt., hdld. (#3500/113)	125.00
Salt & pepper, egg shape, pr.	65.00
Salt & pepper w/chrome tops, pr., ftd. (#34000/77)	45.00
Salt & pepper w/chrome tops, pr., flat (#3900/1177)	35.00
Sandwich tray, center handled (#3400/10)	135.00
Saucer, 3 styles (#3400, #3500, #3900)	7.50
Set: 3 pc. indiv. cream, sug. & tray	60.00
Set: 3 pc. reg. cream, sug. & tray	65.00
Stem, #3121, 1 oz., cordial	65.00
Stem #3121, 3 oz., cocktail	32.50
Stem, #3121, 3½ oz., wine	47.50
Stem, #3121, 4½ oz., claret	45.00
Stem, #3121, 4½ oz., low oyster cocktail	25.00
Stem, #3121, 5 oz., low ft. juice	27.50
Stem, #3121, 5 oz., low ft. parfait	55.00
Stem, #3121, 6 oz., low sherbet	18.00
Stem, #3121, 6 oz., tall sherbet	20.00
Stem, #3121, 10 oz., water	24.00
Stem, #3500, 1 oz., cordial	60.00
Stem, #3500, 2½ oz., wine	37.50
Stem, #3500, 3 oz., cocktail	30.00
Stem, #3500, 4½ oz., claret	33.00
Stem, #3500, 4½ oz., low oyster cocktail	22.50
Stem, #3500, 5 oz., low ft. juice	21.50
Stem, #3500, 5 oz., low ft. parfait	45.00
Stem, #3500, 7 oz., low ft. sherbet	15.00
Stem, #3500, 7 oz., tall sherbet	20.00
Stem, #7801, 4 oz. cocktail, plain stem	40.00
Stem, #7966, 2 oz., sherry, plain ft.	52.50
Sugar, flat	85.00
Sugar, ftd. (#3900/41)	20.00
Sugar, indiv. (#3500/15) pie crust edge	20.00
Sugar, indiv. (#3900/40) scalloped edge	20.00
Tumbler, #3121, 10 oz., low ft. water	21.50
Tumbler, #3121, 12 oz., low ft. ice tea	27.50
Tumbler, #3500, 10 oz., low ft. water	20.00
Tumbler, #3500, 12 oz., low ft. ice tea	23.50
Tumbler, #3900, 5 oz.	40.00
Tumbler, #3900, 13 oz.	42.50
Urn, 10″ (#3500/41)	150.00
Urn, 12″ (#3500/42)	195.00
Vase, 5″, globe (#3400/102)	55.00
Vase, 5″, ftd.	50.00
Vase, 6″, high ftd. flower	55.00
Vase, 8″, flat, flared	65.00
Vase, 8″, high ftd. flower	65.00
Vase, 9″, ftd., keyhole	62.50
Vase, 10″, bud	62.50
Vase, 10″, cornucopia (#3900/575)	100.00
Vase, 10″, flat	95.00
Vase, 10″, ftd.	75.00
Vase, 11″, ftd. flower	85.00
Vase, 11″, ped. ftd. flower	95.00
Vase, 12″, ftd., keyhole	125.00
Vase, 13″, ftd. flower	145.00

SANDWICH, #41, Duncan & Miller Glass Company, 1924 - 1955

Colors: crystal, amber, pink, green, red, cobalt blue

Sandwich was one of Duncan & Miller's largest lines. Only crystal will be priced in this first listing; however, ruby and cobalt are very desirable when found.

	Crystal
Ash tray, 2½″ x 3¾″ rect.	10.00
Ashtray, 2¾″, sq.	8.00
Basket, 6½″ w/loop hdld.	95.00
Basket, 10″, crimped w/loop hdl.	110.00
Basket, 10″, oval w/loop hdl.	110.00
Basket, 11½″, w/loop hdl.	125.00
Bonbon, 5″, heart shape w/ring hdl.	15.00
Bonbon, 5½″, heart shape, hdld.	15.00
Bonbon, 6″, heart shape w/ring hdl.	18.00
Bonbon, 7½″, ftd., w/cover	30.00
Bowl, 2½″, salted almond	7.50
Bowl, 3½″, nut	8.00
Bowl, 4″, finger	12.50
Bowl, 5½″, hdld.	15.00
Bowl, 5½″, ftd. grapefruit w/rim liner	12.00
Bowl, 5½″, ftd. grapefruit w/fruit cup liner . .	12.00
Bowl, 5″, 2 pt. nappy	12.00
Bowl, 5″, ftd., crimped ivy	22.00
Bowl, 5″, fruit	10.00
Bowl, 5″, nappy w/ring hdl.	12.00
Bowl, 6″, 2 pt. nappy	14.00
Bowl, 6″, fruit salad	12.00
Bowl, 6″, grapefruit, rimmed edge	14.00
Bowl, 6″, nappy w/ring hdl.	15.00
Bowl, 10″, salad, deep	50.00
Bowl, 10″, 3 pt., fruit	55.00
Bowl, 10″, lily, vertical edge	40.00
Bowl, 11″, cupped nut	40.00
Bowl, 11½″, crimped flower	45.00
Bowl, 11½″, gardenia	45.00
Bowl, 11½″, ftd., crimped fruit	45.00
Bowl, 12″, fruit, flared edge	35.00
Bowl, 12″, shallow salad	35.00
Bowl, 12″, oblong console	35.00
Bowl, 12″, epergne w/ctr. hole	35.00
Butter w/cover, ¼ lb.	25.00
Cake stand, 11½″, ftd., rolled edge	75.00
Cake stand, 12″, ftd., rolled edge, plain pedestal	60.00
Cake stand, 13″, ftd., plain pedestal	60.00
Candelabra, 10″, 1-lite w/bobeche & prisms . .	40.00

	Crystal
Candelabra, 10″, 3-lite, w/bobeche & prisms .	80.00
Candelabra, 16″, 3-lite w/bobeche & prisms . .	90.00
Candlestick, 4″, 1-lite	12.50
Candlestick, 4″, 1-lite w/bobeche & stub. prisms	22.50
Candlestick, 5″, 3-lite	27.50
Candlestick, 5″, 3-lite w/bobeche & stub. prisms	35.00
Candlestick, 5″, 2-lite w/bobeche & stub. prisms	25.00
Candlestick, 5″, 2-lite	20.00
Candy box w/cover, 5″, flat	28.00
Candy jar w/cover, 8½″, ftd.	40.00
Cheese w/cover (cover 4¾″, plate 8″)	75.00
Cheese/cracker (3″ compote, 13″ plate)	30.00
Cigarette box w/cover, 3½″	20.00
Cigarette holder, 3″, ftd.	25.00
Coaster, 5″	12.00
Comport, 2¼″	14.00
Comport, 3¼″, low ft., crimped candy	16.00
Comport, 3¼″, low ft., flared candy	16.00
Comport, 4¼″, ftd.	18.00
Comport, 5″, low ft.	18.00
Comport, 5½″, ftd., low crimped	20.00
Comport, 6″, low ft., flared	20.00
Condiment set (2 cruets; 3¾″ salt & pepper;	
4 pt. tray)	75.00
Creamer, 4″, 7 oz, ftd.	7.50
Cup, 6 oz., tea	10.00
Epergne, 9″, garden	75.00
Epergne, 12″, 3 pt., fruit or flower	125.00
Jelly, 3″, indiv.	7.00
Mayonnaise set, 3 pc.: Ladle, 5″ bowl, 7″ plate	25.00
Oil bottle, 5¾″	30.00
Pan, 6¾″ x 10½″, oblong camelia	40.00
Pitcher, 13 oz., metal top	40.00
Pitcher w/ice lip, 8″, 64 oz.	95.00
Plate, 3″, indiv. jelly	6.00
Plate, 6″, bread/butter	6.00
Plate, 6½″, finger bowl liner	8.00
Plate, 7″, dessert	7.50
Plate, 8″, mayonnaise liner w/ring	5.00
Plate, 8″, salad	10.00

	Crystal		Crystal
Plate, 9½″, dinner	25.00	Stem, 4¼″, 5 oz., ice cream	12.50
Plate, 11½″, hdld. service	32.50	Stem, 4¼″, 3 oz., wine	18.00
Plate, 12″, torte	40.00	Stem, 5¼″, 4 oz., ftd. parfait	20.00
Plate, 12″, ice cream, rolled edge	40.00	Stem, 5¼″, 5 oz., champagne	20.00
Plate, 12″, deviled egg	55.00	Stem, 6″, 9 oz., goblet	16.50
Plate, 13″, salad dressing w/ring	30.00	Sugar, 3¼″, ftd., 9 oz.	-----
Plate, 13″, service	45.00	Sugar, 5 oz.	7.50
Plate, 13″, service, rolled edge	45.00	Sugar (cheese) shaker, 13 oz., metal top	45.00
Plate, 13″, cracker w/ring	18.00	Tray, oval (for sugar/creamer)	10.00
Plate, 16″, lazy susan w/turntable	65.00	Tray, 6″ mint, rolled edge w/ring hdl.	15.00
Plate, 16″, hostess	60.00	Tray, 7″, oval pickle	15.00
Relish, 5½″, 2 pt., rnd., ring hdl.	12.00	Tray, 7″, mint, rolled edge w/ring hdl.	18.00
Relish, 6″, 2 pt., rnd., ring hdl.	15.00	Tray, 8″, oval	18.00
Relish, 7″, 2 pt. oval	20.00	Tray, 8″, for oil/vinegar	20.00
Relish, 10″, 4 pt. hdld.	22.00	Tray, 10″, oval celery	18.00
Relish, 10″, 3 pt., oblong	25.00	Tray, 12″, fruit epergne	30.00
Relish, 10½″, 3 pt. oblong	25.00	Tray, 12″, ice cream, rolled edge	30.00
Relish, 12″, 3 pt.	35.00	Tumbler, 3¾″, 5 oz., ftd. juice	12.00
Salad dressing set:		Tumbler, 4¾″, 9 oz., ftd. water	14.00
(2 ladles; 5″ ftd. mayonnaise; 13″ plate w/ring)	60.00	Tumbler, 5¼″, 13 oz., flat iced tea	18.00
Salad dressing set:		Tumbler, 5¼″, 12 oz., ftd. iced tea	16.00
(2 ladles; 6″ ftd. div. bowl; 8″ plate w/ring)	50.00	Urn w/cover, 12″, ftd.	75.00
Salt & pepper, 2½″ w/glass tops, pr.	18.00	Vase, 3″, ftd., crimped	12.00
Salt & pepper, 2½″ w/metal tops, pr.	18.00	Vase, 3″, ftd., flared rim	12.00
Salt & pepper, 3¾″ w/metal top (on 6″ tray), 3 pc.	30.00	Vase, 4″, hat shape	15.00
Saucer, 6″, w/ring	4.00	Vase, 4½″, flat base, crimped	15.00
Stem, 2½″, 6 oz., ftd. fruit cup/jello	10.00	Vase, 5″, ftd., flared rim	18.00
Stem, 2¾″, 5 oz., ftd. oyster cocktail	14.00	Vase, 5″, ftd., crimped	18.00
Stem, 3½″, 5 oz., sundae (flared rim)	12.00	Vase, 5″, ftd., fan	25.00
Stem, 4¼″, 3 oz., cocktail	15.00	Vase, 7½″, epergne, threaded base	30.00
		Vase, 10″, ftd.	35.00

123

SATURN, Blank #1485, A. H. Heisey & Co.

Colors: crystal, "Zircon" or "Limelight" green, "Dawn"

"Zircon" was the color name in use from 1937 to 1939. In 1955, this color was remade and called "Limelight".

	Crystal	Zircon/ Limelight
Ash tray	15.00	----
Bitters bottle w/short tube, blown	32.50	
Bowl, baked apple	5.00	42.50
Bowl, finger	4.00	
Bowl, rose, lg.	32.50	
Bowl, 4½", nappy	4.00	
Bowl, 5", nappy	6.00	
Bowl, 5", whipped cream	10.00	47.50
Bowl, 7", pickle	10.00	
Bowl, 9", 3 part relish	15.00	
Bowl, 10", celery	13.00	
Bowl, 11", salad	27.50	
Bowl, 12", fruit, flared rim	30.00	
Bowl, 13", floral, rolled edge	32.50	
Bowl, 13", floral	32.50	
Candelabrum w/"e" ball drops, 2-lite	100.00	285.00
Candle block, 2-lite	90.00	275.00
Candlestick, 3", ftd., 1-lite	12.50	75.00
Comport, 7"	30.00	125.00
Creamer	15.00	85.00
Cup	9.00	44.00
Hostess Set, 8 pc. (low bowl w/ftd. ctr. bowl, 3 toothpick holders and clips)	50.00	175.00
Marmalade w/cover	30.00	
Mayonnaise	17.50	50.00
Mustard w/cover and paddle	35.00	225.00
Oil bottle, 2 oz., w/#1 stoppper	45.00	210.00
Parfait, 5 oz.	9.00	42.00
Pitcher, 70 oz., w/ice lip, blown	52.50	200.00
Pitcher, juice	30.00	225.00
Plate, 6"	3.00	15.00
Plate, 7", bread	5.00	25.00
Plate, 8", luncheon	7.00	35.00
Plate, 13", torte	15.00	
Plate, 15", torte	20.00	
Salt & pepper, pr.	35.00	350.00
Saucer	3.00	16.00
Stem, 3 oz., cocktail	6.00	45.00
Stem, 4 oz., fruit cocktail	5.00	40.00
Stem, 4½ oz., sherbet	5.00	40.00
Stem, 5 oz., sherbet	5.00	40.00
Stem, 6 oz., saucer champagne	7.00	50.00
Stem, 10 oz.	10.00	70.00
Sugar	15.00	85.00
Sugar shaker	35.00	
Sugar w/cover, no handles	20.00	
Tray, tid bit, 2 sides turned as fan	20.00	70.00
Tumbler, 5 oz., juice	4.00	60.00
Tumbler, 7 oz., old fashioned	6.00	
Tumbler, 8 oz., old fashioned	7.00	
Tumbler, 9 oz., luncheon	8.00	
Tumbler, 10 oz.	10.00	
Tumbler, 12 oz., soda	12.00	45.00
Vase, violet	20.00	60.00
Vase, 8½", flared	25.00	160.00
Vase, 8½", straight	25.00	160.00

"SPIRAL FLUTES", Duncan & Miller Glass Company, Introduced 1924

Colors: amber, green, pink

A prominent Michigan collector says that the 72 pieces listed here are complete, so I'll take his word for now. If anyone has a piece we do not have listed, I certainly want to know. There are three items that are extremely plentiful: 6¾" flanged bowls, 7½" plates and 7 oz. footed tumblers

Since there are only a few collectors of this pattern now, this might be a pattern to start searching for in your travels.

	Amber, Green, Pink		Amber, Green, Pink
Bowl, 2", almond	8.00	Ice tub, handled	30.00
Bowl, 3¾", bouillion	12.00	Lamp, 10½", countess	150.00
Bowl, 4⅜", finger	5.00	Mug, 6½", 9 oz., handled	25.00
Bowl, 4¾", ftd. cream soup	15.00	Mug, 7", 9 oz., handled	30.00
Bowl, 4" w., mayonnaise	15.00	Oil w/stopper, 6 oz.	100.00
Bowl, 5", nappy	5.00	Pickle, 8⅝"	12.00
Bowl, 6½", cereal, sm. flange	12.50	Pitcher, ½ gal.	95.00
Bowl, 6¾", grapefruit	7.50	Plate, 6", pie	3.00
Bowl, 6", handled nappy	20.00	Plate, 7½", salad	4.00
Bowl, 6", handled nappy w/cover	50.00	Plate, 8⅜", luncheon	4.00
Bowl, 7", nappy	15.00	Plate, 10⅜", dinner	20.00
Bowl, 7½", flanged (baked apple)	20.00	Plate, 13⅝", torte	25.00
Bowl, 8", nappy	15.00	Plate w/star, 6", (fingerbowl liner)	6.00
Bowl, 8½", flanged (oyster plate)	20.00	Platter, 11"	25.00
Bowl, 9", nappy	25.00	Platter, 13"	35.00
Bowl, 10", oval veg.	35.00	Relish, 10" x 7⅞", oval, 3 pc. (2 inserts)	45.00
Bowl, 10½", lily pond	35.00	Saucer	3.00
Bowl, 11¾" w. x 3¾" t., console, flared	25.00	Saucer, demi	5.00
Bowl, 11", nappy	25.00	Seafood sauce cup, 3" w. x 2½" h.	20.00
Bowl, 12", cupped console	25.00	Stem, 3¾", 3½ oz. wine	15.00
Candle, 3½"	12.50	Stem, 3¾", 5 oz., low sherbet	8.00
Candle, 7½"	40.00	Stem, 4¾", 6 oz., tall sherbet	12.00
Candle, 9½"	45.00	Stem, 5⅝", 4½ oz., parfait	15.00
Candle, 11½"	75.00	Stem, 6¼", 7 oz., water	15.00
Celery, 10¾" x 4¾"	15.00	Sugar, oval	8.00
Chocolate jar w/cover (crystal)	125.00	Sweetmeat w/cover, 7½"	65.00
Cigarette holder, 4"	30.00	Tumbler, 3⅜", ftd., 2½ oz., cocktail (no stem)	7.00
Comport, 4⅜"	15.00	Tumbler, 4¼", 8 oz., flat	25.00
Comport, 6⅝"	17.50	Tumbler, 4⅜", ftd., 5½ oz., juice (no stem)	14.00
Comport, 9", low ft., flared	45.00	Tumbler, 4¾", 7 oz., flat soda	25.00
Console stand, 1½" h. x 4⅝" w.	12.00	Tumbler, 5⅛", ftd., 7 oz. water (1 knob)	8.00
Creamer, oval	8.00	Tumbler, 5⅛", ftd., 9 oz. water (no stem)	17.50
Cup	9.00	Tumbler, 5½", 11 oz., gingerale	25.00
Cup, demi	20.00	Vase, 6½"	10.00
Fernery, 10" x 5½", 4 ft. flower box	150.00	Vase, 8½"	15.00
Grapefruit, ftd.	20.00	Vase, 10½"	20.00

TEAR DROP, #301, Duncan & Miller Glass Company, 1936 - 1955

Colors: crystal

Another of Duncan & Miller's very popular patterns for many years was Tear Drop. You will find a few of these crystal pieces with colored handles. At today's prices, this may be one of the best buys in a crystal pattern listed in this book.

	Crystal		Crystal
Ash tray, 3″ indiv.	6.00	Coaster/ashtray, 3″, rolled edge	7.00
Ashtray, 5″	8.00	Comport, 4¾″, ftd.	12.00
Bonbon, 6″ 4 hdld.	10.00	Comport, 6″, low foot. hdld.	15.00
Bottle w/stopper, 12″, bar	75.00	Condiment set: 5 pc. (salt/pepper, 2 3oz. cruets,	
Bowl, 4¼″, finger	7.00	9″, 2 hdld. tray)	65.00
Bowl, 5″, fruit nappy	6.00	Creamer, 3 oz.	5.00
Bowl, 5″, 2 hdld. nappy	8.00	Creamer, 6 oz.	6.00
Bowl, 6″, dessert nappy	6.00	Creamer, 8 oz.	8.00
Bowl, 6″, fruit nappy	6.00	Cup, 2½ oz., demi	10.00
Bowl, 7″, fruit nappy	7.00	Cup, 6 oz. tea	6.00
Bowl, 7″, 2 hdld. nappy	10.00	Flower basket, 12″, loop hand.	65.00
Bowl, 8″ x 12″, oval flower	30.00	Ice bucket, 5½″	45.00
Bowl, 9″, salad	25.00	Marmalade w/cover, 4″	30.00
Bowl, 9″, 2 hdld. nappy	20.00	Mayonnaise, 4½″ (2 hdld. bowl, ladle, 6″ plate)	27.50
Bowl, 10″, crimped console, 2 hdld.	25.00	Mayonnaise set, 3 pc. (4½″ bowl, ladle, 8″	
Bowl, 10″, flared fruit	25.00	hdld. plate)	32.50
Bowl, 11½″, crimped flower	30.00	Mustard jar w/cover, 4¼″	30.00
Bowl, 11½″, flared flower	30.00	Nut dish, 6″, 2 pt.	10.00
Bowl, 12″, salad	32.50	Oil bottle, 3 oz.	17.50
Bowl, 12″, crimped, low foot	35.00	Olive dish, 4¼″, 2 hdld. oval	15.00
Bowl, 12″, ftd. flower	40.00	Olive dish, 6″, 2 pt.	15.00
Bowl, 12″, sq., 4 hdld.	40.00	Pickle dish, 6″	15.00
Bowl, 13″, gardenia	35.00	Pitcher, 5″, 16 oz., milk	40.00
Bowl, 15½″, 2½ gal. punch	75.00	Pitcher, 8½″, 64 oz., w/ice lip	75.00
Butter w/cover, ¼ lb., 2 hdld.	22.00	Plate, 6″, bread/butter	4.00
Cake salver, 13″, ftd.	35.00	Plate, 6″, canape	10.00
Canape set: (6″ plate w/ring, 4 oz., ftd. cocktail)	20.00	Plate, 7″, 4 hdld., lemon	12.50
Candlestick, 4″	9.00	Plate, 7½″, salad	5.00
Candlestick, 7″, 2-lite, ball loop ctr.	15.00	Plate, 8½″, luncheon	7.00
Candlestick, 7″, lg. ball ctr. w/bobeches, prisms	22.50	Plate, 10½″, dinner	20.00
Candy basket, 5½″ x 7½″, 2 hdld. oval	45.00	Plate, 11″, 2 hdld.	27.50
Candy box w/cover, 7″, 2 pt., 2 hdld.	30.00	Plate, 13″, 4 hdld.	25.00
Candy box w/cover, 8″, 3 pt., 3 hdld.	35.00	Plate, 13″, rolled edge salad liner	25.00
Candy dish, 7½″, heart shape	20.00	Plate, 13″, torte, rolled edge	27.50
Celery, 11″, 2 hdld.	15.00	Plate, 14″, torte	30.00
Celery, 11″, 2 pt., 2 hdld.	18.00	Plate, 14″, torte, rolled edge	30.00
Celery, 12″, 3 pt.	20.00	Plate, 16″, torte, rolled edge	32.50
Cheese & cracker (3½″ comport, 11″ 2		Plate, 18″, lazy susan	35.00
hdld. plate)	35.00	Plate, 18″, punch liner, rolled edge	35.00

	Crystal		Crystal
Relish, 7″, 2 pt., 2 hdld.	15.00	Sugar, 8 oz.	8.00
Relish, 7½″, 2 pt. heart shape	18.00	Sweetmeat, 5½″, star shape, 2 hdld.	20.00
Relish, 9″, 3 pt., 3 hdld.	22.50	Sweetmeat, 6½″, ctr. hdld.	22.50
Relish, 11″, 3 pt. 2 hdld.	25.00	Sweetmeat, 7″, star shape, 2 hdld.	22.50
Relish, 12″, 3 pt.	25.00	Tray, 5½″, ctr. hdld. (for mustard jar)	10.00
Relish, 12″, 5 pt. rnd.	25.00	Tray, 6″, 2 hdld. (for salt/pepper)	10.00
Relish, 12″, 6 pt., rnd.	25.00	Tray, 7¾″, ctr. hdld. (for cruets)	12.50
Relish, 12″, sq., 4 pt., 4 hdld.	25.00	Tray, 8″, 2 hdld. (for oil/vinegar)	12.50
Salad set, 6″ (compote, 11″ hdld. plate)	35.00	Tray, 8″, 2 hdld. (for sugar/creamer)	7.50
Salad set, 9″, (2 pt. bowl, 13″ rolled edge plate)	55.00	Tray, 10″, 2 hdld (for sugar/creamer)	8.00
Salt & pepper, 5″	25.00	Tumbler, 2¼″, 2 oz., flat whiskey	12.50
Saucer, 4½″, demi	3.00	Tumbler, 2¼″, 2 oz., ftd. whiskey	12.50
Saucer, 6″	1.50	Tumbler, 3″, 3 oz., ftd. whiskey	12.50
Stem, 2½″, 5 oz., ftd. sherbet	5.00	Tumbler, 3¼″, 3½ oz., flat juice	8.00
Stem, 2¾″, 3½ oz., ftd. oyster cocktail	7.50	Tumbler, 3¼″, 7 oz., flat old fashioned	10.00
Stem, 3½″, 5 oz. sherbet	6.00	Tumbler, 3½″, 5 oz., flat juice	8.00
Stem, 4″, 1 oz., cordial	25.00	Tumbler, 4″, 4½ oz., ftd. juice	9.00
Stem, 4½″, 1¾ oz., sherry	25.00	Tumbler, 4¼″, 9 oz., flat	9.00
Stem, 4½″, 3½ oz., cocktail	20.00	Tumbler, 4½″, 8 oz., flat split	9.00
Stem, 4¾″, 3 oz., wine	22.00	Tumbler, 4½″, 9 oz., ftd.	9.00
Stem, 5″, 5 oz., champagne	12.50	Tumbler, 4¾″, 10 oz., flat hi-ball	10.00
Stem, 5½″, 4 oz., claret	15.00	Tumbler, 5″, 8 oz., ftd. party	10.00
Stem, 5¾″, 9 oz.	12.50	Tumbler, 5¼″, 12 oz., flat iced tea	12.50
Stem, 6¼″, 8 oz., ale	15.00	Tumbler, 5¾″, 14 oz., flat hi-ball	14.00
Stem, 7″, 9 oz.	15.00	Tumbler, 6″, 14 oz., iced tea	15.00
Sugar, 3 oz.	5.00	Urn w/cover, 9″, ftd.	75.00
Sugar, 6 oz.	6.00	Vase, 9″, ftd. fan	20.00
		Vase, 9″, ftd. round	25.00

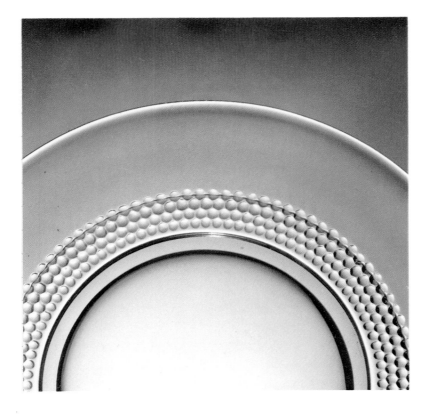

TROJAN, Fostoria Glass Company, 1929 - 1944

Colors: "Rose" pink, "Topaz" yellow; some green seen

Pink Trojan is quite scarce; therefore it is the yellow that is the more collectible. Difficult items to locate include footed oils and the combination bowl, which is a bowl having candle holders on each end serving as handles. Pitchers and unclouded shakers are prized items also.

	Rose, Topaz		Rose, Topaz
Ash tray, lg.	27.50	Oyster, cocktail, ftd.	22.50
Ash tray, sm.	22.50	Parfait	35.00
Bowl, 9", baker	37.50	Pitcher	265.00
Bowl, bonbon	12.50	Plate, canape	15.00
Bowl, bouillon, ftd.	15.00	Plate, 6", bread/butter	5.00
Bowl, cream soup, ftd.	17.50	Plate, 6¼", finger bowl liner	6.50
Bowl, finger w/6¼" liner	22.00	Plate, 7½", salad	7.50
Bowl, lemon	15.00	Plate, 7½", cream soup liner	7.50
Bowl, mint	15.00	Plate, 8¾", , luncheon	10.00
Bowl, 5", fruit	15.00	Plate, 9½", sm. dinner	16.00
Bowl, 6", cereal	20.00	Plate, 10", cake, handled	25.00
Bowl, 7", soup	22.50	Plate, 10¼", grill, rare	35.00
Bowl, lg. dessert, handled	29.50	Plate, 10¼", dinner	32.50
Bowl, 10"	29.00	Plate, 13", chop	37.50
Bowl, combination w/candleholder handles	100.00	Platter, 12"	32.50
Bowl, 12" centerpiece, sev. types	33.50	Platter, 15"	50.00
Candlestick, 2"	13.00	Relish, 8½"	15.00
Candlestick, 3"	15.00	Relish, 3 pt.	22.00
Candlestick, 5"	19.50	Sauce boat	40.00
Candy w/cover, ½ lb.	97.50	Sauce plate	15.00
Celery, 11½"	21.50	Saucer, after dinner	7.50
Cheese & cracker, set	42.50	Saucer	4.50
Comport, 6"	25.00	Shaker, ftd., pr.	70.00
Comport, 7"	27.50	Sherbet, 6", high	20.00
Creamer, ftd.	17.50	Sherbet, 4¼", low	16.00
Creamer, tea	35.00	Sugar, ftd.	17.50
Cup, after dinner	27.50	Sugar cover	75.00
Cup, ftd.	16.00	Sugar pail	90.00
Goblet, claret, 6", 4 oz.	35.00	Sugar, tea	35.00
Goblet, cocktail, 5¼", 3 oz.	25.00	Sweetmeat	13.50
Goblet, cordial, 4", ¾ oz.	62.50	Tray, 11", ctr. hdld.	32.50
Goblet, water, 8¼", 10 oz.	27.50	Tray, service	27.50
Goblet, wine, 5½", 3 oz.	40.00	Tray, service & lemon	32.50
Grapefruit	40.00	Tumbler, 2½ oz., ftd.	25.00
Grapefruit liner	35.00	Tumbler, 5 oz., ftd., 4½"	22.50
Ice bucket	65.00	Tumbler, 9 oz., ftd., 5¼"	15.50
Ice dish	27.50	Tumbler, 12 oz., ftd., 6"	20.00
Ice dish liner (tomato, crab, fruit)	7.00	Vase, 8"	110.00
Mayonnaise w/liner	30.00	Whipped cream bowl	11.00
Oil, ftd.	225.00	Whipped cream pail	95.00

Note: See page 69 for stem identification.

TWIST, Blank #1252, A. H. Heisey & Co.

Colors: crystal, "Flamingo" pink, "Moongleam" green; "Marigold" amber/yellow; some "Sahara", a florescent yellow and some "Alexandrite", (rare)

	Crystal	Pink	Green	Marigold Sahara
Baker, 9″, oval	10.00	15.00	20.00	45.00
Bonbon	5.00	10.00	15.00	20.00
Bonbon, 6″, 2 hdld.	5.00	10.00	15.00	20.00
Bottle, French dressing	20.00	55.00	75.00	105.00
Bowl, cream soup/bouillon	15.00	25.00	30.00	50.00
Bowl, ftd. almond/indiv. sugar	15.00	30.00	35.00	60.00
Bowl, indiv. nut	5.00	20.00	25.00	45.00
Bowl, 4″, nappy	5.00	12.00	15.00	17.00
Bowl, 6″, 2 hdld.	7.00	15.00	17.00	20.00
Bowl, 6″, 2 hdld. jelly	7.00	15.00	17.00	20.00
Bowl, 6″, 2 hdld. mint	7.00	15.00	17.00	20.00
Bowl, 8″, low ftd.	20.00	30.00	35.00	65.00
Bowl, 8″, nappy, grnd. bottom	12.00	18.00	25.00	40.00
Bowl, 8″, nasturtium, rnd.	20.00	28.00	35.00	60.00
Bowl, 8″, nasturtium, oval	20.00	28.00	35.00	60.00
Bowl, 9″, floral	22.00	30.00	37.00	62.00
Bowl, 9″, floral, rolled edge	22.00	30.00	37.00	62.00
Bowl, 12″, floral, oval, 4 ft.	25.00	32.00	40.00	65.00
Bowl, 12″, floral, rnd., 4 ft.	25.00	32.00	40.00	65.00
Candlestick, 2″, 1-lite	7.50	10.00	12.50	20.00
Cheese dish, 6″, 2 hdld.	5.00	10.00	15.00	20.00
Comport, 7″, tall	25.00	50.00	65.00	130.00
Creamer, hotel oval	15.00	35.00	40.00	50.00
Creamer, individual (unusual)	10.00	25.00	30.00	55.00
Creamer, zig-zag handles, ftd.	20.00	30.00	35.00	60.00
Cup, zig-zag handles	10.00	25.00	30.00	35.00
Grapefruit, ftd.	10.00	15.00	20.00	30.00
Ice tub	25.00	60.00	65.00	90.00
Pitcher, 3 pint	35.00	80.00	125.00	------
Mayonnaise	15.00	20.00	25.00	40.00
Mayonnaise #1252½	15.00	22.50	30.00	50.00
Mustard w/cover	25.00	50.00	65.00	90.00
Oil bottle, 2½ oz., w/#78 stopper	30.00	60.00	75.00	100.00
Oil bottle, 4 oz., w/#78 stopper	35.00	65.00	80.00	110.00
Plate, cream soup liner	5.00	7.00	10.00	15.00
Plate, 8″, Kraft cheese	15.00	25.00	35.00	55.00
Plate, 8″, grnd. bottom	7.00	12.00	15.00	20.00
Plate, 10″, utility, 3 ft.	20.00	30.00	40.00	-----
Plate, 12″, 2 hdld. sandwich	20.00	35.00	45.00	55.00
Plate, 12″, muffin, 2 hdld., turned sides	20.00	40.00	50.00	65.00
Plate, 13″, 3 part relish	10.00	15.00	20.00	35.00
Platter, 12″	15.00	35.00	45.00	70.00
Salt & pepper, 2 styles	30.00	55.00	95.00	95.00
Saucer	3.00	5.00	7.00	10.00
Stem, 2½ oz., wine	15.00	25.00	30.00	35.00
Stem, 3 oz., oyster cocktail	5.00	15.00	20.00	25.00
Stem, 3 oz., cocktail	5.00	15.00	20.00	25.00
Stem, 5 oz., saucer champagne	7.00	16.00	20.00	25.00
Stem, 5 oz., sherbet	7.50	12.00	17.50	22.50
Stem, 9 oz., luncheon (1 block in stem)	15.00	20.00	30.00	40.00
Sugar, ftd.	20.00	30.00	35.00	60.00
Sugar, hotel oval	15.00	35.00	40.00	50.00
Sugar, individual (unusual)	15.00	30.00	35.00	60.00
Sugar w/cover, zig-zag handles	15.00	25.00	35.00	65.00
Tray, 7″, pickle, grnd. bottom	7.00	15.00	20.00	25.00
Tray, 10″, celery	10.00	20.00	25.00	30.00
Tray, 13″, celery	12.00	25.00	35.00	45.00
Tumbler, 5 oz., fruit	4.00	12.00	18.00	24.00
Tumbler, 6 oz., ftd. soda	5.00	13.00	19.00	25.00
Tumbler, 8 oz., flat, grnd. bottom	7.00	15.00	20.00	30.00
Tumbler, 8 oz., soda, straight & flared	7.00	15.00	20.00	30.00
Tumbler, 9 oz., ftd. soda	8.00	16.00	21.00	31.00
Tumbler, 12 oz., iced tea	11.00	22.00	27.50	42.50
Tumbler, 12 oz., ftd. iced tea	12.00	25.00	30.00	45.00

VERSAILLES, Fostoria Glass Company, 1928 - 1944

Colors: blue, yellow, pink, green

Versailles is one of the Fostoria patterns most highly prized by the modern day collectors. The company gave the center handled server and the candy dish a fleur de lis "handle" to further connect the glass with its namesake.
As is true of June, the pitcher and footed oils are choice pieces to own.
Notice that only the bowls of the stemware are colored. The stems are crystal, something often done by glass makers.
The whipped cream pail will have a nickle plated handle; but the salad dressing bottle comes with a sterling top.

	Pink, Green	Blue	Yellow		Pink, Green	Blue	Yellow
Ash tray	24.00	30.00	25.00	Ice dish liner (tomato, crab, fruit)	5.00	10.00	7.50
Bottle, salad dressing with sterling top	250.00	------	300.00	Mayonnaise w/liner	35.00	50.00	40.00
Bowl, 9", baker	30.00	45.00	40.00	Oil, ftd.	225.00	325.00	250.00
Bowl, bonbon	12.00	18.00	14.00	Oyster cocktail	20.00	27.50	22.00
Bowl, bouillon, ftd.	16.00	22.00	18.00	Parfait	27.50	35.00	30.00
Bowl, cream soup, ftd.	16.00	24.00	20.00	Pitcher	250.00	350.00	275.00
Bowl, finger w/liner	20.00	27.50	25.00	Plate, 6", bread/butter	4.00	5.00	4.00
Bowl, lemon	11.00	18.00	14.00	Plate, 7½", salad	6.00	8.00	7.00
Bowl, mint	14.00	20.00	16.00	Plate, 7½", cream soup liner	6.00	8.00	7.00
Bowl, 5", fruit	14.00	17.50	15.00	Plate, 8¾", , luncheon	8.00	10.00	9.00
Bowl, 6", cereal	20.00	25.00	22.00	Plate, 9½", sm. dinner	14.00	17.50	15.00
Bowl, 7", soup	25.00	32.50	30.00	Plate, 10", grill	20.00	30.00	25.00
Bowl, lg. dessert, 2 hdld. . . .	27.50	35.00	30.00	Plate, 10", cake, 2 hdld.	26.00	35.00	30.00
Bowl, 10"	30.00	35.00	32.00	Plate, 10¼", dinner	35.00	42.00	37.50
Bowl, 11", centerpiece	30.00	37.50	35.00	Plate, 13", chop	30.00	40.00	35.00
Bowl, 12", centerpiece, sev. type	22.50	42.50	35.00	Platter, 12"	30.00	40.00	35.00
Bowl, 13", oval centerpiece	35.00	47.50	40.00	Platter, 15"	50.00	65.00	50.00
Candlestick, 2"	15.00	17.50	16.00	Relish, 8½"	30.00	40.00	35.00
Candlestick, 3"	16.00	20.00	17.50	Sauce boat	40.00	60.00	45.00
Candlestick, 5"	20.00	25.00	22.00	Sauce plate	12.00	20.00	15.00
Candy w/cover, 3 pt.	65.00	100.00	85.00	Saucer, after dinner	4.00	6.00	5.00
Candy w/cover, ½ lb.	55.00	95.00	75.00	Saucer	4.00	6.00	5.00
Celery, 11½"	30.00	40.00	50.00	Shaker, ftd., pr.	80.00	110.00	85.00
Cheese & cracker, set	45.00	60.00	50.00	Sherbet, high, 6"	20.00	25.00	22.50
Comport, 6"	23.00	32.00	27.50	Sherbet, low, 4¼"	20.00	24.00	22.00
Comport, 7"	25.00	35.00	30.00	Sugar, ftd.	15.00	20.00	15.00
Comport, 8"	30.00	40.00	35.00	Sugar cover	85.00	125.00	95.00
Creamer, ftd.	15.00	20.00	15.00	Sugar pail	80.00	125.00	90.00
Creamer, tea	27.50	30.00	27.50	Sugar, tea	27.50	30.00	27.50
Cup, after dinner	25.00	40.00	30.00	Sweetmeat	12.00	17.50	14.00
Cup, ftd.	17.50	21.00	19.00	Tray, 11", ctr. hdld.	25.00	35.00	30.00
Decanter	175.00	250.00	200.00	Tray, service	30.00	40.00	35.00
Goblet, cordial, 4", ¾ oz. . .	60.00	75.00	65.00	Tray, service & lemon	32.50	42.50	37.50
Goblet, claret, 6", 4 oz.	40.00	65.00	45.00	Tumbler, 2½ oz., ftd.	30.00	37.50	35.00
Goblet, cocktail, 5¼", 3 oz. . .	25.00	32.50	28.00	Tumbler, 5 oz., ftd., 4½" . . .	20.00	25.00	22.00
Goblet, water, 8¼", 10 oz. .	27.50	32.50	30.00	Tumbler, 9 oz., ftd., 5¼" . . .	20.00	25.00	21.50
Goblet, wine, 5½", 3 oz. . . .	35.00	50.00	42.00	Tumbler, 12 oz., ftd., 6" . . .	22.50	27.50	25.00
Grapefruit	40.00	50.00	40.00	Vase, 8"	100.00	135.00	110.00
Grapefruit liner	30.00	35.00	30.00	Vase, 8½", fan, ftd.	60.00	85.00	65.00
Ice bucket	62.50	80.00	75.00	Whipped cream bowl	12.00	15.00	13.00
Ice dish	30.00	40.00	30.00	Whipped cream pail	70.00	90.00	80.00

Note: For stem identification see page 69.

VESPER, Fostoria Glass Company, 1926 - 1934

Colors: amber, green, some blue

	Green	Amber	Blue
Ash tray	20.00	25.00	
Bowl, finger	15.00	17.50	
Bowl, ftd., bouillon	12.00	15.00	
Bowl, cream soup	12.50	14.00	
Bowl, 5½", fruit	8.00	10.00	15.00
Bowl, 6½", cereal	14.00	17.50	20.00
Bowl, 7¾", soup, shallow	15.00	17.50	25.00
Bowl, 8", soup, deep	16.00	18.50	
Bowl, 8"	20.00	22.50	
Bowl, 9"	25.00	27.50	
Bowl, 11", console	22.50	25.00	
Bowl, 13", console	22.50	25.00	
Candlestick, 2"	12.50	12.50	
Candlestick, 4"	15.00	15.00	30.00
Candlestick, 9"	15.00	17.50	50.00
Candy jar w/cover	60.00	75.00	125.00
Candy jar, ftd. w/cover	100.00	125.00	
Cheese, ftd.	18.00	20.00	
Comport, 6"	22.50	25.00	35.00
Comport, 7"	25.00	28.00	40.00
Comport, 8"	35.00	40.00	50.00
Creamer, ftd.	14.00	16.00	
Creamer, fat, ftd.	18.00	20.00	25.00
Cup	12.00	14.00	
Cup, after dinner	18.00	20.00	35.00
Dish, celery	15.00	17.50	
Finger bowl liner, 6"	4.50	5.50	
Grapefruit	35.00	35.00	
Grapefruit liner	25.00	30.00	
Ice bucket	50.00	55.00	
Oyster cocktail	16.00	18.00	
Pitcher, ftd.	275.00	295.00	
Plate, 6", bread/butter	4.50	5.00	
Plate, 7½", salad	6.00	6.50	
Plate, 8½", luncheon	7.50	8.50	
Plate, 9½", sm. dinner	10.00	11.00	
Plate, 10½", dinner	22.00	27.50	
Plate, 11", ctr. hand.	22.50	25.00	
Plate, 13", chop	32.00	37.50	
Plate, 15", server	35.00	40.00	
Plate w/indent for cheese	18.00	20.00	
Platter, 10½"	21.50	23.50	
Platter, 12"	30.00	35.00	
Platter, 15"	40.00	45.00	
Salt & pepper, pr., 2 styles	60.00	67.50	
Sauce boat w/liner	65.00	75.00	
Saucer, after dinner	7.50	9.00	15.00
Saucer	4.00	4.50	
Stem, sherbet	15.00	16.00	
Stem, water	22.50	25.00	
Stem, low sherbet	14.00	15.00	
Stem, parfait	25.00	27.50	
Stem, ¾ oz., cordial	60.00	65.00	
Stem, 2½ oz., ftd.	20.00	22.50	
Stem, 2¾ oz., wine	22.50	25.00	
Stem, 3 oz., cocktail	22.50	25.00	
Sugar, fat ftd.	18.00	20.00	25.00
Sugar, ftd.	14.00	16.00	
Sugar, lid	125.00	125.00	
Tumbler, 5 oz., ftd.	14.00	15.00	
Tumbler, 9 oz., ftd.	15.00	16.00	
Tumbler, 12 oz., ftd.	18.00	20.00	
Urn, sm.	45.00	50.00	
Urn, lg.	60.00	70.00	110.00
Vase, 8"	60.00	65.00	90.00

NOTE: Page 69 for stem identification.

WAVERLY, Blank #1519, A. H. Heisey & Co.

Colors: crystal; rare in amber

	Crystal
Bowl, 6″, oval lemon w/cover	25.00
Bowl, 6½″, 2 hdld. ice	45.00
Bowl, 7″, 3 part relish, oblong	25.00
Bowl, 7″, salad	20.00
Bowl, 9″, 4 part relish, round	22.50
Bowl, 9″, fruit	30.00
Bowl, 9″, vegetable	30.00
Bowl, 10″, crimped edge	15.00
Bowl, 10″, gardenia	15.00
Bowl, 11″, seahorse foot, floral	57.50
Bowl, 12″, crimped edge	37.50
Bowl, 13″, gardenia	20.00
Box, 5″, chocolate w/cover	35.00
Box, 5″ tall, ft. w/cover, seahorse hand.	62.50
Box, 6″, candy w/bow tie knob	32.50
Box, trinket, lion cover (rare)	1,100.00
Butter dish w/cover, 6″, square	50.00
Candleholder, 1-lite, block (rare)	125.00
Candleholder, 2-lite	20.00
Candleholder, 2-lite, "flame" center	50.00
Candleholder, 3-lite	50.00
Candle epergnette, 5″	7.50
Candle epergnette, 6″, deep	12.50
Candle epergnette, 6½″	9.00
Cheese dish, 5½″, ft.	6.00
Cigarette holder	30.00
Comport, 6″, low ft.	6.00
Comport, 6½″, jelly	8.00
Comport, 7″, low ft., oval	28.00
Creamer, ft.	15.00
Creamer & sugar, individual w/tray	30.00
Cruet, 3 oz., ft. w/#122 stopper	40.00
Cup	10.00
Honey dish, 6½″, ft.	7.00
Mayonnaise w/liner & ladle, 5½″	25.00
Plate, 7″, salad	4.00
Plate, 8″, luncheon	6.00
Plate, 10½″, server	20.00
Plate, 11″, sandwich	12.00
Plate, 13½″, ft. cake salver	45.00
Plate, 14″, center handle sandwich	45.00
Plate, 14″, sandwich	20.00
Salt & pepper, pr.	25.00
Saucer	3.00
Stem, 1 oz., cordial	95.00
Stem, 3 oz., wine, blown	55.00
Stem, 3½ oz., cocktail	32.50
Stem, 5½ oz., sherbet/champagne	15.00
Stem, 10 oz., blown	20.00
Sugar, ft.	15.00
Tray, 12″, celery	13.00
Tumbler, 5 oz., ft. juice, blown	15.00
Tumbler, 13 oz., ft. tea, blown	20.00
Vase, 3½″, violet	25.00
Vase, 7″, ft.	22.00
Vase, 7″, ft., fan shape	25.00

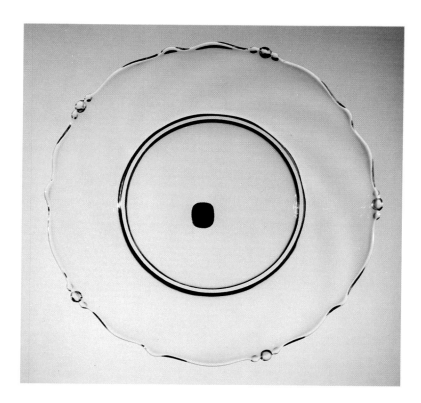

141

WILDFLOWER, Cambridge Glass Company, 1940's - 1950's

Colors: crystal, mainly; some few pieces in color

Wildflower in color shows up occasionally and is highly desirable. It would be very difficult to collect a set in color, and most collectors are happy enough to find it in crystal. Price the colored items 25% to 30% above the crystal prices listed.

	Crystal		Crystal
Basket, 6", 2 hdld. ftd.	20.00	Plate, 8", salad	11.00
Bowl, 5¼", 2 hdld., bonbon	15.00	Plate, 10½", dinner	40.00
Bowl, 6", 2 hdld. ftd. bonbon	16.50	Plate, 12", 4 ftd. service	30.00
Bowl, 6", 2 pt. relish	17.50	Plate, 13", 4 ftd. torte	32.50
Bowl, 6½", 3 pt. relish	17.50	Plate, 13½", 2 hdld. cake	32.50
Bowl, 7", relish	17.50	Plate, 14", torte	35.00
Bowl, 7", 2 hdld. bonbon	19.00	Salt & pepper, pr.	30.00
Bowl, 7", 2 pt. relish	17.50	Saucer	3.50
Bowl, 8", 3 hdld. 3 pt. relish	25.00	Set: 2 pc. Mayonnaise (ft. sherbet	
Bowl, 9", 3 pt. celery & relish	25.00	w/ladle)	22.50
Bowl, 9½", ftd. pickle (corn)	22.00	Set: 3 pc. Mayonnaise (bowl, liner,	
Bowl, 10", 4 ft. flared	30.00	ladle)	25.00
Bowl, 11", 2 hdld	30.00	Set: 4 pc. Mayonnaise (div. bowl,	
Bowl, 11½", ftd. w/tab hand.	32.50	liner, 2 ladles)	30.00
Bowl, 12", 3 pt. celery & relish	30.00	Stem, #3121, 1 oz., cordial	47.50
Bowl, 12", 4 ft. flared	29.50	Stem, #3121, 3 oz., cocktail	22.50
Bowl, 12" 4 ft. oval, "ears" hand.	40.00	Stem, #3121, 3½ oz. wine	25.00
Bowl, 12", 5 pt celery & relish	35.00	Stem, #3121, 4½ oz. claret	22.00
Candlestick, 3-lite, ea.	30.00	Stem, #3121, 4½ oz., low oyster	
Candlestick, 5"	22.50	cocktail	16.00
Candlestick, 6", 2-lite "fleur de lis"	27.50	Stem, #3121, 5 oz., low parfait	22.50
Candy box w/cover, 8", 3 hdld. 3 pt.	52.50	Stem, #3121, 6 oz. low sherbet	15.00
Candy box w/cover, rnd.	47.50	Stem, #3121, 6 oz. tall sherbet	17.50
Cocktail icer, 2 pc.	25.00	Stem, #3121, 10 oz. water	20.00
Comport, 5½"	27.50	Sugar	12.50
Comport, 5⅜", blown	37.50	Sugar, indiv.	12.50
Creamer	12.50	Tumbler, #3121, 5 oz., juice	12.50
Creamer, indiv.	12.50	Tumbler, #3121, 10 oz., water	15.00
Cup	16.50	Tumbler, #3121, 12 oz., tea	17.50
Hurricane lamp, candlestick base	100.00	Tumbler, 13 oz.	20.00
Hurricane lamp, keyhole base & prisms	120.00	Vase, 5", globe	27.50
Ice bucket w/chrome hand.	55.00	Vase, 6", ftd. flower	27.50
Oil, 6 oz. w/stopper	40.00	Vase, 8", ftd. flower	30.00
Pitcher, ball	95.00	Vase, 9", keyhole ft.	37.50
Pitcher, Doulton	135.00	Vase, 10", bud	25.00
Plate, 6", 2 hdld.	12.50	Vase, 11", ftd. flower	37.50
Plate, 6½", bread/butter	7.50	Vase, 11", ped. ft.	42.50
Plate, 8", 2 hdld. bonbon	17.50	Vase, 12", keyhole ft.	47.50
Plate, 8", 2 hdld. ftd.	20.50	Vase, 13", ftd. flower	60.00

Note: See Pages 148-149 for stem identification.

YEOMAN, Blank #3184, A. H. Heisey & Co.

Colors: crystal, "Flamingo" pink, "Sahara" yellow, "Moongleam" green; "Hawthorne" orchid/pink; "Marigold" deep, amber/yellow; some cobalt

Empress etched pieces of Yeoman will fetch 10% to 20% more than the prices listed below.

	Crystal	Pink	Sahara	Green	Hawth.	Marigold
Ash tray, 4″, hdld. (bow tie).............	10.00	17.00	19.00	22.00	25.00	27.00
Bowl, 2 hdld. cream soup................	10.00	15.00	20.00	23.00	27.00	30.00
Bowl, finger	5.00	10.00	14.00	18.00	22.00	26.00
Bowl, ftd., banana split.................	7.00	20.00	25.00	30.00	35.00	40.00
Bowl, ftd., 2 hdld. bouillon	10.00	20.00	25.00	30.00	35.00	40.00
Bowl, 4½″, nappy	4.00	7.00	10.00	12.00	14.00	15.00
Bowl, 5″, low ftd. jelly	12.00	20.00	25.00	27.00	30.00	37.00
Bowl, 5″, oval lemon...................	7.00	10.00	14.00	17.00	19.00	23.00
Bowl, 5″, rnd. lemon...................	6.00	10.00	14.00	17.00	19.00	23.00
Bowl, 5″, rnd. lemon w/cover	11.00	15.00	20.00	25.00	30.00	35.00
Bowl, 6″, oval preserve.................	7.00	12.00	17.00	22.00	27.00	30.00
Bowl, 6″, vegetable	5.00	10.00	14.00	16.00	19.00	24.00
Bowl, 6½″, hdld. bonbon	5.00	10.00	14.00	16.00	19.00	24.00
Bowl, 8″, rect. pickle/olive	12.00	15.00	20.00	25.00	30.00	35.00
Bowl, 8½″, berry, 2 hdld	14.00	19.00	24.00	29.00	34.00	40.00
Bowl, 9″, 2 hdld. veg. w/cover	25.00	35.00	45.00	55.00	75.00	100.00
Bowl, 9″, oval fruit	20.00	25.00	35.00	45.00	50.00	55.00
Bowl, 9″, baker	20.00	25.00	35.00	45.00	50.00	55.00
Bowl, 12″, low floral...................	15.00	25.00	35.00	45.00	50.00	55.00
Cigarette box, (ash tray cover)...........	25.00	35.00	45.00	55.00	65.00	75.00
Cologne bottle w/stopper	40.00	75.00	80.00	85.00	90.00	120.00
Comport, 5″, high ftd., shallow	15.00	25.00	35.00	45.00	55.00	65.00
Comport, 6″, low ftd., deep	20.00	30.00	34.00	38.00	42.00	48.00
Creamer.............................	10.00	15.00	17.00	19.00	22.00	28.00
Cruet, 2 oz. oil	20.00	35.00	40.00	45.00	50.00	55.00
Cruet, 4 oz. oil	25.00	37.50	42.50	47.50	52.50	60.00
Cup	5.00	15.00	20.00	25.00	30.00	40.00
Cup, after dinner	7.00	20.00	25.00	30.00	35.00	40.00
Egg cup	15.00	22.00	30.00	37.00	40.00	50.00
Grapefruit, ftd........................	10.00	17.00	24.00	31.00	38.00	45.00
Gravy (or dressing) boat w/underliner	13.00	18.00	23.00	28.00	33.00	40.00
Marmalade jar w/cover.................	25.00	35.00	40.00	45.00	50.00	65.00
Parfait, 5 oz..........................	10.00	15.00	20.00	25.00	30.00	35.00
Pitcher, quart	35.00	45.00	55.00	65.00	100.00	130.00
Plate, 2 hdld. cheese	5.00	10.00	13.00	15.00	17.00	25.00
Plate, cream soup underliner............	5.00	7.00	9.00	12.00	14.00	16.00
Plate, finger bowl underliner	3.00	5.00	7.00	9.00	11.00	13.00
Plate, 4½″, coaster....................	3.00	5.00	10.00	12.00		
Plate, 6″.............................	3.00	6.00	8.00	10.00	13.00	15.00
Plate, 6″, bouillon underliner...........	3.00	6.00	8.00	10.00	13.00	15.00

145

	Crystal	Pink	Sahara	Green	Hawth.	Marigold
Plate, 6½″, grapefruit bowl	7.00	12.00	15.00	18.00	25.00	30.00
Plate, 7″	5.00	8.00	10.00	13.00	15.00	20.00
Plate, 8″, oyster cocktail	9.00					
Plate, 8″, soup	9.00					
Plate, 9″, oyster cocktail	10.00					
Plate, 10½″	12.00					
Plate, 10½″, ctr. hand. oval, div.	15.00	25.00		30.00		
Plate, 11″, 4 pt. relish	20.00	26.00		30.00		
Plate, 14″	20.00					
Platter, 12″, oval	10.00	17.00	19.00	26.00	32.00	
Salt, ind. tub (cobalt: $20.00)	5.00	7.00		12.00		
Salver, 10″, low ftd.	15.00	25.00		40.00		
Salver, 12″, low ftd.	10.00	20.00		30.00		
Saucer	3.00	5.00	7.00	7.00	10.00	10.00
Saucer, after dinner	3.00	5.00	7.00	8.00	10.00	10.00
Stem, 2¾ oz., ftd. oyster cocktail	3.00	5.00	7.00	8.00	12.00	
Stem 3 oz., cocktail	7.00	12.00	17.00	20.00		
Stem, 3½ oz., sherbet	5.00	8.00	10.00	12.00		
Stem, 4 oz., fruit cocktail	3.00	5.00	7.00	9.00		
Stem, 4½ oz., sherbet	3.00	5.00	7.00	9.00		
Stem, 5 oz., soda	4.00	6.00	8.00	10.00		
Stem, 5 oz., sherbet	3.00	5.00	7.00	9.00		
Stem, 6 oz., champagne	6.00	11.00	16.00	18.00		
Stem, 8 oz.	5.00	10.00	15.00	17.00		
Stem, 10 oz., goblet	7.00	12.00	17.00	19.00		
Stem, 12 oz., tea	8.00	14.00	19.00	22.00		
Sugar w/cover	12.00	22.00	25.00	27.00	30.00	35.00
Sugar shaker, ftd.	30.00	85.00		90.00		
Syrup, 7 oz., saucer ftd.	25.00	55.00				
Tray, 7″ x 10″, rect.	26.00	30.00	38.00	35.00		
Tray, 9″, celery	10.00	14.00	16.00	15.00		
Tray, 11″, ctr. hand., 3 pt.	15.00	18.00	22.00			
Tray, 12″, oblong	16.00	19.00	24.00			
Tray, 13″, 3 pt. relish	20.00	26.00	30.00			
Tray, 13″, celery	20.00	26.00	30.00			
Tray, 13″, hors d'oeuvre w/cov. ctr.	30.00	40.00	50.00	65.00		
Tray insert, 3½″ x 4½″	4.00	6.00	7.00	8.00		
Tumbler, 2½ oz., whiskey	3.00	5.00	7.00	9.00		
Tumbler, 4½ oz., soda	4.00	6.00	10.00	15.00		
Tumbler, 8 oz.	4.00	12.00	17.00	20.00		
Tumbler, 8 oz.	4.00	12.00	17.00	20.00		
Tumbler, 10 oz., cupped rim	4.00	15.00	20.00	22.00		
Tumbler, 10 oz., straight side	5.00	15.00	20.00	22.00		
Tumbler, 12 oz., tea	5.00	16.00	22.00	24.00		
Tumbler cover (unusual)	25.00					

CAMBRIDGE STEMS

1066
11 oz. Goblet

1402
Brandy Inhaler (Tall)

3025
10 oz. Goblet

3035
3 oz. Cocktail

3077
6 oz. Tall Sherbet

3104
1 oz. Cordial

3106
9 oz. Goblet Tall Bowl

3115
3½ oz. Cocktail

3120
6 oz. Tall Sherbet

3121
10 oz. Goblet

148

CAMBRIDGE STEMS

3122
9 oz. Goblet

3124
3 oz. Wine

3126
7 oz. Tall Sherbet

3130
6 oz. Tall Sherbet

3135
6 oz. Tall Sherbet

3400
9 oz. Lunch Goblet

3500
10 oz. Goblet

3600
2½ oz. Wine

3775
4½ oz. Claret

3625
4½ oz. Claret

3779
1 oz. Cordial

149

CAMBRIDGE'S RARITIES

Candy, crystal, CHANTILLY 120.00
Pitcher, emeral green, GLORIA 350.00
Pitcher, yellow, PORTIA 600.00
Pitcher, Heatherbloom, PORTIA 600.00
Pitcher, Moonlight blue, CLEO 150.00
Pitcher, alpine crystal, CAPRICE 135.00
Pitcher, small crystal, ROSEPOINT 155.00
Pitcher, pink tankard, APPLEBLOSSOM 195.00
Pitcher, amber Doulton, GLORIA 400.00
Pitcher, pink ball juice, DIANE 425.00
Tumbler, crystal old fashioned, ROSEPOINT 80.00

HEISEY'S RARITIES

Bowl, fern, "Zircon" color, dolphin handle 125.00

Butter, ¼ lb., "Dawn" color 150.00

Candle block, Lariat blank (1540), one pair known to date 125.00

Candy, amber color, Waverly blank (1519) 350.00

Creamer & sugar, "Vaseline" color 450.00

Creamer & sugar, "Hawthorne w/Moongleam handles" 450.00

Creamer & sugar, crystal, cut and signed by Krall 1,000.00

Goblet, "Alexandrite" color, Creole blank, wine 140.00

Mug, cobalt 300.00

Pitcher, "Moongleam" color, Ipswich blank 500.00

Pitcher, "Orchid" tankard 450.00

Pitcher, "Flamingo" color, Optic Tooth blank #4206 . . . .   150.00

Plate, black, Lariat blank (1540) 1,200.00

Plate, "Tangerine" color, Empress 130.00

Relish, "Zircon" color, Whirlpool blank (1506) 175.00

Vase, "Flamingo" color, Optic Tooth blank (4206) 80.00

HEISEY'S "ALEXANDRITE" COLOR (rare)

Bowl, 12″, floral, Twist (1252) 265.00
Candlesticks, pr. (134) 500.00
Cream & sugar, pr., Empress (1401) 400.00
Compote, Albermarle (3368) 125.00
Cup & saucer, Queen Ann (1509) 125.00
Jelly, 6″, w/dolphin feet Queen Ann (1509) 90.00
Mayonnaise w/dolp. ft. & ladle Queen Ann (1509) 185.00
Plate, 8″, Empress (1401) 60.00
Salt & pepper, pr. Queen Ann (1509) 235.00
Stem, 2½ oz. wine, Creole (3381) 140.00
Stem, 2½ oz. wine, Old Dominion (3380) 110.00
Stem, 6 oz. champagne, Old Dominion (3380) 75.00
Stem, 11 oz. water goblet Carcassone (3390) 80.00
Stem 11 oz. water goblet Creole (3381) 135.00
Vase, 4″, ball Wide Optic (4045) 200.00

HEISEY'S "ALEXANDRITE" COLOR (rare)

Ash tray, Empress (1401)	130.00
Candlestick, 7″, pr. (135)	350.00
Celery tray, 10″, Empress (1401)	150.00
Nut, individual, Empress (1401)	80.00
Plate, 6″, square, Empress (1401)	35.00
Plate, 7″, square, Empress (1401)	45.00
Plate, 8″, square, Empress (1401)	60.00
Plate, 10″, square, Empress (1401)	125.00
Tumbler, 1 oz., cordial, Carcassonne (3390)	100.00
Tumbler, 2½ oz., bar, Glenford (3481)	100.00
Tumbler, 5 oz. ftd. soda, Creole (3381)	60.00
Tumbler, 8½ oz., ftd. soda, Creole (3381)	50.00
Tumbler, 12 oz., ftd. soda, Creole (3381)	60.00
Vase, 9″, ftd., Empress (1401)	525.00

HEISEY'S "COBALT" COLOR (rare)

Ash tray, Empress (1401)	125.00
Ash tray or butter pat Old Sandwich (1404)	30.00
Bowl, 12″, Thumbprint & Panel (1433)	100.00
Candlestick, pr., Thumbprint & Panel (1433)	200.00
Cigarette holder, Carcassonne (3390)	85.00
Creamer, 12 oz., Old Sandwich (1404)	260.00
Mug, 12 oz., Old Sandwich	275.00
Plate, 8″, round, Queen Ann (1509)	50.00
Plate, 8″, square, Empress, (1401)	60.00
Salt & pepper shaker pr. (24)	95.00
Salt tub, individual, Revere (1183)	90.00
Stem, 1 oz., cordial, Spanish stem (3404)	165.00
Stem, 2½ oz., wine, Carcassonne (3390)	110.00
Stem, 3½ oz., cocktail, Spanish stem (3404)	60.00
Stem 4 oz., claret, Spanish stem (3404)	125.00
Stem 5½ oz. sherbet Spanish stem (3404)	65.00
Stem, 6 oz., sherbet, Carcassonne (3390)	80.00
Stem 8 oz., ftd. soda, Spanish stem (3404)	95.00
Stem, 11 oz., low ftd. goblet, Carcassonne (3390)	90.00
Stem, 12 oz., ftd. soda, Carcassonne (3390)	60.00
Tumbler, 9 oz., Arch (1417)	65.00
Vase, 2″ ball, Wide Optic (4045)	400.00
Vase, 4″ ball, Wide Optic (4045)	115.00
Vase, 9″, pr., Warwick (1428)	350.00
Vase, 9″ ftd. tulip (1420)	325.00
Vase, favor, Diamond Optic (4228)	75.00
Vase, favor, Diamond Optic (4230)	75.00
Vase, ivy, Wide Optic (4224)	140.00

HEISEY'S "DAWN" COLOR (rare)

Ash tray, 5¼" Lodestar (1632) 65.00
Ash tray, Prism Square (1593) 75.00
Bowl, 6¾" jelly (1565) 37.50
Bowl, crimped, Lodestar (1626) 85.00
Candy, 5" w/cover Lodestar (1632) 110.00
Cruet, 3 oz., crys. stopper Saturn (1483) 225.00
Jar & cover, Lodestar (1626) 175.00
Pitcher, 1 qt., Lodestar (1626) 100.00
Relish, 12", 4 pt., Octagon (500) 225.00
Salt shaker, Saturn (1485) 65.00
Sherbet, 20th Century (1415) 30.00
Tumbler, Coleport (1487) 35.00
Tumbler, 6 oz., Lodestar (1632) 30.00
Vase, 7½", Lodestar (1626) 130.00

HEISEY'S TANGERINE COLOR (rare)

Plate, 8″, Empress blank (1401)	130.00
Stem, champagne Duquesne blank (3389)	175.00
Stem, cocktail Gascony (3397) looks red	225.00
Stem, sherbet Duquesne blank (3389)	165.00
Stem, water Duquesne blank (3389)	190.00
Tumbler, ice tea Spanish stem (3404)	400.00
Tumbler, juice Duquesne blank (3389)	125.00
Tumbler, soda Gascony (3397) looks red	300.00
Vase, favor (4232)	400.00
Vase, ivy	200.00

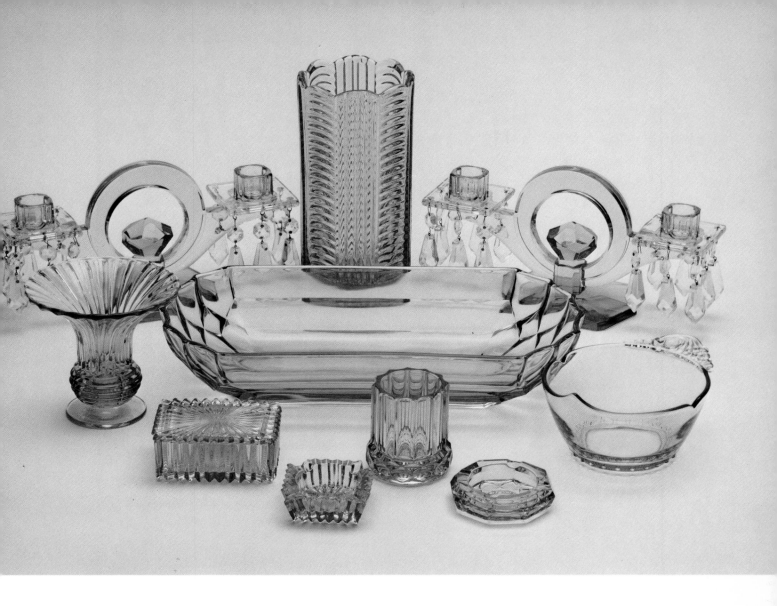

HEISEY'S ZIRCON (LIMELIGHT) COLOR (rare)

Ash tray, Kohinoor (1488). 80.00
Ash tray, Ridgeleigh (1469). 35.00
Bowl, 6″, hdld. jelly, Fern (1495). 45.00
Bowl, 13″, floral, Kohinoor (1488). 350.00
Cigarette box, Ridgeleigh (1469) 150.00
Cigarette holder, Kohinoor (1488) 200.00
Candelabra pr., Kohinoor (1488) 900.00
Candle vase, Ridgeleigh (1469). 75.00
Vase, 8″, Ridgeleigh (1469½) 145.00

Publications I recommend

DEPRESSION GLASS DAZE

THE ORIGINAL NATIONAL DEPRESSION GLASS NEWSPAPER

Depression Glass Daze, the Original, National monthly newspaper dedicated to the buying, selling and collecting of colored glassware of the 20's and 30's. We average 60 pages each month, filled with feature articles by top notch columnists, readers "finds", club happenings, show news, a china corner, a current listing of new glass issues to beware of and a multitude of ads! You can find it in the DAZE! Keep up with what's happening in the dee gee world with a subscription to the DAZE. Buy sell or trade from the convenience of your easy chair.

Name_____ Street_____

City_____ State_____ Zip_____

☐ 1 Year - $15.00   ☐ Check enclosed   ☐ Please bill me

☐ MasterCard   ☐ VISA   (Foreign subscribers - please add $1.00 per year)

Exp. date_____Card No._____

Signature_____

Orders to D.G.D., Box 57GF, Otisville, MI 48463-008 - Please allow 30 days

GLASS review

A colorful magazine devoted to keeping glass collectors informed about all kinds of glass - antique to contemporary collectibles. Filled with articles, pictures, price reports, ads, research information and more! 12 "BIG" issues yearly.

Name_____ Street_____

City_____ State_____ Zip_____

☐ New   ☐ 1 year - $14.50   ☐ Single Copy $2.00

☐ Renewal   ☐ 1 year Canada or Foreign $16.00 (U.S. Funds please)

Orders to P. O. Box 542, Marietta, OH 45750

Heisey Club Membership To:

Heisey Collectors of America
Box 27GF
Newark, OH 43055
Dues: $12.00 Yearly

Books by Gene Florence

Pocket Guide To Depression Glass, Fourth Edition

by Gene Florence
ISBN: 0-89145-279-6

Gene Florence has updated all the current values in America's favorite *Pocket Guide to Depression Glass* in this new fourth edition. We have re-photographed over 50% of the patterns and added the new finds making this an all new book, not just a revised edition. This full color presentation is in the same easy-to-use format with bold photographs that make pattern identification simple. A special section on reproductions is included to help the collector differentiate between authentic Depression Glass and the modern reproductions and reissues. This pocket guide is a must for both the beginner and advanced collector.

5½ x 8½, 160 Pages, Paperback $9.95

Kitchen Glassware of the Depression Years 2nd Edition

by Gene Florence
ISBN: 0-89145-237-0

Kitchen Glassware has consistantly been on our top 10 bestseller list since it was published in June 1981. Now this new second edition will be even better. This second edition is 50% larger and totally revised and updated. This edition is a totally new book with over 80% of the photos being new and all values updated. Thousands of pieces of glass are featured in full color in this large 192-page, 8½ x 11, hardbound volume. It includes canisters, salt & pepper shakers, reamers, strawholders, containers, pitchers and many other miscellaneous kitchen pieces.

8½ x 11, 192 Pages, Hardbound $19.95

The Collector's Encyclopedia of Occupied Japan Collectibles
by Gene Florence
ISBN: 0-89145-002-1
During the occupation after World War II, most items manufactured in Japan were marked "Made in Occupied Japan". These include ceramics, toys, games, wooden items, leather, and lots more. This beautiful, full color volume explores many of these items and places current values on them. Updated 1982 values.
8½ x 11, 108 Pages, Hardbound $12.95

Collectors Encyclopedia of Depression Glass, 7th Edition

by Gene Florence
ISBN: 0-89145-306-4

Depression Glass is still the most popular glassware collected today. This new 7th edition of that ever popular glassware will be bigger and better than ever. This new 7th edition features all the new finds that have turned up since the 6th edition plus adds many new group shots as well as updates all the values on all the popular pieces in each pattern. This full color volume features over 5,000 pieces of glass listing size, color, pattern description and current market value. Now with over 325,000 copies in print, it is one of the best selling price guides on the market today. A section is devoted to exposing re-issues and fakes, alerting the unknowing buyer as to what has been released and how to determine the old valuable glass from the worthless new issues.

Gene Florence is the country's most respected authority on Depression Glass.

8½ x 11, 224 Pages, Hardbound $19.95

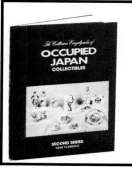

The Collector's Encyclopedia of Occupied Japan Collectibles II
by Gene Florence
ISBN: 0-89145-111-0
The first edition of Occupied Japan collectibles was so popular that many new finds surfaced and there became a need for a companion volume. This full color hardbound volume features photographs of hundreds of pieces with no repeats from the first book. Current values, updated for 1982, are given for each item.
8½ x 11, 112 Pages, Hardbound $12.95

Copies of these books may be ordered from:

Gene Florence
P.O. Box 22186
Lexington, KY 40522

COLLECTOR BOOKS
P.O. Box 3009
Paducah, KY 42001

Add $1.00 postage for the first book, $.35 for each additional book.

Two Important Tools For The
Astute Antique Dealer, Collector and Investor

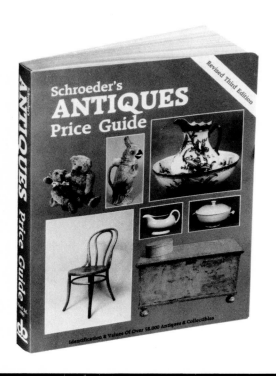

Schroeder's Antiques Price Guide

The very best low cost investment that you can make if you are really serious about antiques and collectibles is a good identification and price guide. We publish and highly recommend **Schroeder's Antiques Price Guide.** Our editors and writers are very careful to seek out and report accurate values each year. We do not simply change the values of the items each year but start anew to bring you an entirely new edition. If there are repeats, they are by chance and not by choice. Each huge edition (it weighs 3 pounds!) has over 56,000 descriptions and current values on 608 - 8½x11 pages. There are hundreds and hundreds of categories and even more illustrations. Each topic is introduced by an interesting discussion that is an education in itself. Again, no dealer, collector or investor can afford not to own this book. It is available from your favorite bookseller or antiques dealer at the low price of $9.95. If you are unable to find this price guide in your area, it's available from Collector Books, P. O. Box 3009, Paducah, KY 42001 at $9.95 plus $1.00 for postage and handling.

Schroeder's INSIDER and Price Update

A monthly newsletter published for the antiques and collectibles marketplace.

The **"INSIDER"**, as our subscribers have fondly dubbed it, is a monthly newsletter published for the antiques and collectibles marketplace. It gives the readers timely information as to trends, price changes, new finds, and market moves both upward and downward. Our writers are made up of a panel of well-known experts in the fields of Glass, Pottery, Dolls, Furniture, Jewelry, Country, Primitives, Oriental and a host of other fields in our huge industry. Our subscribers have that "inside edge" that makes them more profitable. Each month we explore 8-10 subjects that are "in", and close each discussion with a random sampling of current values that are recorded at press time. Thousands of subscribers eagerly await each monthly issue of this timely 16-page newsletter. A sample copy is available for $3.00 postpaid. Subscriptions are $24.00 for 12 months; 24 months for $45.00; 36 months for $65.00, all postpaid. A sturdy 3-ring binder to store your **Insider** is available for $5.00 postpaid. This newsletter contains NO paid advertising and is not available on your newsstand. It may be ordered by sending your check or money order to Collector Books, P. O. Box 3009, Paducah, KY 42001.

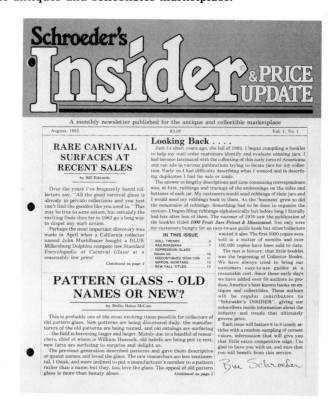